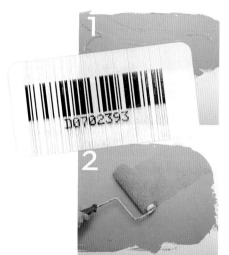

THE
DECORATING
CHALLENGE

THE DECORATING

THE DECORATING CHALLENGE TEAM
with **Sheri Craig**

CHALLENGE

NETWORK

PHOTOGRAPHY **Tom Tkach**

Dedicated to the memory of our friend Scott Olson.

ROOM TEXT Sheri Craig
HOW-TO TEXT Scott Olson
EDITED Alison Maclean
PROOFREAD Marial Shea
COVER AND INTERIOR DESIGN Stacey Noyes / luzform design
PHOTOGRAPHS Tom Tkach Photography

Printed and bound in Hong Kong

NATIONAL LIBRARY OF CANADA CATALOGUING IN PUBLICATION DATA

Craig, Sheri
    The decorating challenge / the Decorating Challenge team with Sheri Craig.

    ISBN 1-55285-352-7

    1. Interior decoration. 2. Dwellings--Remodeling. 3. Decorating challenge (Television program)
    I. Title.
NK2115.C72 2003   747   C2002-911458-6

The publisher acknowledges the support of the Canada Council for the Arts and the Cultural Services Branch of the Government of British Columbia for our publishing program. We acknowledge the financial support of the Government of Canada through the Book Publishing Industry Development Program for our publishing activities.

CONTENTS

THE DECORATING CHALLENGE I still find it hard to believe that *The Decorating Challenge* has been a part of my life now for six years. It was in the fall of 1997 that my daughter Courtney and I made the pilot show for what today is *The Decorating Challenge.*

It all came together one evening when we had a few friends over for dinner. My husband and I starting throwing out funny and quirky ideas of what one could put into a decorating show; then our friends got into the act. The most important element, we decided, was the budget. We wanted to create a program that would help viewers create dramatic effects with limited funds. The makeovers also had to be do-able for ordinary folk who might, or might not, be handy types. A time limit would add drama and entertainment value to the show. So, armed with these three main ideas: inexpensive, easy, and quick makeovers, we mapped out a pilot.

At first we thought we could do a makeover in twelve hours. Well, were we surprised! On the first day we were painting walls and eating Chinese food at midnight. We also found out that the homeowners should live within ten minutes of each other. We hadn't thought of that, so for the pilot our poor host was in the car driving between the houses for the better part of two days. Did she put a lot of mileage on her car!

It is always useful to do a pilot because that way you can see what works and what doesn't. When we eventually sold the show to the Women's Television Network we had tweaked it and ironed out most of the bumps, though with this show there are always surprises. Each show has its own personality, much depends on the charisma of the homeowners and the look that the designer wants to achieve. Our interior designers are great and over the years we have worked with them until, finally, I think we can say we have figured out how

UPCOUNTRY AMBIANCE

much we can do in one weekend. Some of the designers have been known to be too ambitious at times. But that's where our amazing carpenters come in. Not only are they extremely talented, they're the nicest people you could ever wish to meet. When they say, "This is too ambitious," the designers listen. The carpenters are our reality checkers.

Our host, Renée Montpellier, is a delightful young woman, and she is just as nice in person as she is on camera. Renée is the one who takes the participants under her wing and helps them get over their nervousness.

There are many other terrific people who work behind the scenes on the television show and without whose support we couldn't do it. We have makeup artists who not only do their jobs well but are also good painters, sanders, and tea makers. Kudos also to the camera and audio operators who have been known to pitch in and help with the occasional carpentry project or electrical problem.

We have a lot of fun making this television series even though it is sometimes very stressful. On a personal note, I would like to thank my daughter Courtney who has hung in there with me through thick and thin (and sometimes I am a bossy mum.) The other person I would like to thank is producer Scott Olson who does tremendous work and without whom this book would have been difficult to complete.

VYVYAN CAMPBELL
J. V. PRODUCTIONS —
SEPTEMBER 2002

THE CHALLENGE When Michelle Butterly and Carl Hanstke came home each day, they walked into a dark front hall. Their 1920s house had gumwood panelling in the downstairs hall and wood on the floor, stairs, spindles, banisters and landings. "We want our front hall to make a statement," said Michelle. "Right now you walk in and say, 'Oh look, wood.'" Added Carl, "We want to feel at ease when we walk in. We're at home, relax and cut back." They knew the entrance to their home should be warmer and more friendly. But they were also quite emphatic, "Don't paint the wood."

MAKING A STATEMENT

THE GOAL To brighten the vestibule, downstairs hall, stairs and landing, providing more character to the front entrance of the house. But could this be done with all that dark wood?

THE TEAM Michelle and Carl's neighbours Peter and Rosanna Mohr, with designer Christine Newell and carpenter Bill Crossman.

FRONT HALL

THE SOLUTION Although Christine knew she would have trouble with her other team members, she was convinced that the wood panelling would have to be painted. "It was necessary to bring the remaining wood to life," she explained. She chose CIL Dulux low lustre satin Golden Spa (30YY 57/342) for the ceiling and walls and Orion latex eggshell (40 YY 75/216), a slightly darker shade, for the panelling.

BEFORE **WOOD PANELLING**   AFTER **PAINTED WOOD PANELLING**

DAY 1

PAINTING The crew, with some trepidation, began painting. First they washed the panelling to remove any nicotine or wax build-up, then they applied primer in vertical strokes to create a smooth finish. When the primer dried the panelling would be ready to be painted.

SHELVING Since there was no room for furniture in the hall or on the landing, Christine decided to create some display space, claiming part of the upstairs linen closet to make a built-in shelving unit for accessories. There were also two old-fashioned radiators to cover, providing two more handy shelves. While Bill, working inside, made the first cut for the shelving unit, Peter was outside starting on the first radiator cover. (See how-to box.)

SPECIAL TOUCHES Renée came across Christine surrounded by a handful of small, rather plain shades. "I bought a chandelier at a garage sale for $15," explained Christine. "I've sprayed and distressed it and now I'm going to use these shades, after I tape over the images we want to preserve, and spray paint the rest gold. They'll look good on top." Renée volunteered to tape while Christine went to find Bill who had his wall shelf insert ready for framing. By the end of Day One, Rosanna agreed that painting the panelling had been a good idea. "It looks amazing," she said.

HOW TO EASY RADIATOR COVER

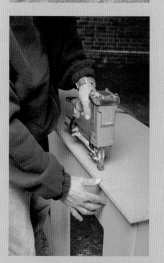

tape measure

table saw or skill saw

carpenter's glue

hammer and nails

router with bits

jig saw

drill

³/₄-inch MDF

wood filler

spatula

wire mesh

square

paint

12 metal L-brackets with screws

staple gun

wire cutters

Measure the radiator that you would like to cover.

Cut the MDF into four pieces according to the dimensions of the rad and the following instructions. For the rad front, the MDF piece should measure the width plus 6 inches by the height plus 2 inches. The side pieces should match the depth of the radiator from the wall plus 2 inches by the height of the radiator plus 2 inches.

For the rad top, cut one solid piece measuring the width of the rad plus 8 inches by the depth of the rad from the wall + 3 ³/₄ inches. This should give the top a 1-inch lip around the top and sides. The back should line up flush.

Dry fit the structure. The two side pieces should abut the inside of the front pieces so that the sides are flush to the outside edge of the front piece.

To allow heat to escape, the rad cover must have outlet holes. Leaving a good 6 to 8 inches from the side, centre and draw three equal squares along the front of the front piece. Using the drill and the jig-saw, cut out the squares. You may also draw and cut decorative details along the bottom and sides of the cover. Rout the outside edge of all the cut-outs. Rout the sides and the front edge of the top piece leaving the back edge flush.

Measure and cut out the wire mesh so that it completely covers the square holes on the front piece, leaving an edge to staple to the MDF. Staple the mesh in place on the inside of the front piece.

To assemble, apply a generous amount of carpenter's glue to the side and front joins. Place the side piece so that it abuts the inside of the front piece, making sure that the side is flush to the outside edge of the front piece. Nail together from the front. Repeat for the other side/front pieces.

Secure the cover by installing two metal L-brackets on the inside of each joint.

Put the top in place and attach it using the remaining L-brackets.

Fill all nail holes with wood filler. Let dry, sand and paint.

DAY 2

FINISHING Christine was busy with the second coat of paint while Bill measured up as he readied the radiator cover for routering. After Bill completed the frames for the radiator covers, he attached mesh in front of the panels to hide the plywood cuts and then framed the mesh with trim. (See how-to box, previous page.) Meanwhile, Rosanna was working on a faux plaster wall plaque, another garage sale find, using gold cream to give it an antique look.

CRACKLING Christine, definitely a super bargain shopper, had bought a large wall clock at a second hand shop for $10. She painted it white, intending to give it a crackle finish. Renée said she had done crackle before so she got the job. (See how-to box.)

WINDOW TREATMENT The large window on the landing would be the focal point of the design. Christine bought French toile fabric in mustard and blue, which Rosanna used to make elegant floor-to-ceiling curtains. The blue was repeated in peel-and-stick floor tiles in the vestibule and in candle holders that Christine made out of old wall sconces.

SPECIAL TOUCHES As a grand finale, Peter laid a royal blue carpet runner, which also matched the blue in the curtains, down the stairs, fixing the runner to the stair treads with shiny brass rods. This gave the hall entrance a sense of Victoriana, which characterized the overall feel of the home, Christine said.

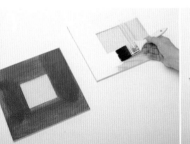

HOW TO CRACKLE FINISH

sandpaper

soft cloth

liquid crackle medium

acrylic paint — a darker colour for the base coat and lighter colour for the top coat

paintbrushes

antiquing medium

Minwax or diluted brown or yellow ochre paint.

Crackle finish is ideal for wooden pieces such as picture frames or wooden doors, since wood allows the finish to really stand out.

Sand the wood so that the surface is smooth and any existing finish is completely removed. Wipe the entire surface with a soft cloth.

Paint one or two coats of the darker base coat. Let dry completely.

Apply the crackle medium using smooth, even strokes and covering the piece completely. Touch up missed spots immediately, covering only the missed areas so that the overall smoothness of the stroke isn't marred.

Paint the lighter coloured topcoat paint over the crackle medium.

Streaks and uneven spots will develop into a crackled, antique-like finish as the medium dries.

This final step isn't absolutely necessary, but it helps pull the effect together. Rub antiquing medium, diluted brown or yellow ochre paint or min-wax into the antiqued surface with a soft cloth until you achieve an attractive effect.

TIP Thick coats of paint will produce large cracks after the antiquing medium has dried; thinner coats of paint will produce smaller cracks; and sponged-on paint will create tiny, delicate cracks such as those seen on fine antique china.

THE RESULT When Michelle and Carl saw their hallway, they couldn't believe they were in the same house. "We told you not to paint the wood, but thank goodness you did," said Michelle. Christine said while she doesn't believe there any basic rules for decorating, in this instance fabric made a big impact on the overall design. "But people should trust their instincts and do what they love in a room."

BUDGET

Drapery Fabric	$198.06	Spray Paint	$20.00
Stair Runner	$185.27	Candle Holder/Candles/Trivet	$18.28
Brass Rods for Stair Runner	$53.00	Light Cylinders	$14.18
Brackets/Ivy Plant/Vase	$51.65	Metal Mesh	$11.00
Floor Tiles	$50.00	Clock (from Goodwill)	$10.80
Vase/Wooden Plaque (from second hand store)	$49.68	Crackle Glaze	$6.66
		Fabric Headings	$2.59
Lights/Lampshades/Pots/ Planters (from second hand store)	$33.48	Screws	$1.35
		Carpenter's Expenses	$120.19
Rings for Drapes	$31.21		

TOTAL (EXCLUDING PAINT)   **$857.40**

THE CHALLENGE Margot and Mark Sommerville's home is a suburban house with an open concept living and dining room area, leading off into the foyer and hall. They had painted the space yellow but were not happy with the shade. The room was furnished with a dining set, a couch and a chair and not much else to pull it together. The Sommervilles envisioned an upmarket country feel, a setting that didn't include stencilling, floral wallpaper, gingham or sponge painting. Other than that they were open to all ideas and wanted some help.

UPCOUNTRY AMBIANCE

THE GOAL Create a warm, sophisticated, adult space that is also childproof. The room should be yellow, but the right shade of yellow!

THE TEAM Neighbours Wayne and Grace Price, with designer Ellie Cholette and carpenter Jeremy Plant.

LIVING ROOM

THE SOLUTION Ellie decided that the space was perfect, especially since it included two pillars for architectural detail, but it needed some pizzazz that she would create with colour. So, assembling her team, Ellie began by using the yellow that was already there as a base coat, and added texture with CIL Dulux Cypress, a soft latex eggshell green (70YY 33/243). She showed Wayne and Grace how to smoosh, applying paint with glaze and sheets of plastic (see how-to box). "There's a whole lot of smooshing going on," said Renée.

BEFORE DULL PALE YELLOW   AFTER WARM SMOOSHED WALLS WITH DRAMATIC RED ACCENTS

DAY 1

WAINSCOTING Meanwhile, Jeremy was carefully measuring and then cutting and installing wainscoting in the hall and foyer. He had a full agenda because after the wainscoting, Ellie wanted him to put cornice molding around the ceiling.

WALLS Back to the smooshing and the colour was coming on strong. The Prices called it "pea soup green" and wondered how the Somervilles would like it, but Ellie was confident and adamant. She knew her problem would be to pull the whole open area together, keeping each space as its own entity, and showing off the pillars. She had the Somervilles' yellow but still needed a strong colour in the hall. She also wanted to have some fun with colour. Her idea was to select Salsa (10YR 14/348), a rich, dark red that would add spunk and give the area a modern and trendy look. To keep the space bright, the pillars and the walls under the wainscoting were painted latex eggshell Natural White (50YY 83/029).

Grace seemed hesitant at first, but she rose to the challenge as she rolled on the Salsa red. "Oh this is needed, very much needed," she said. "I really like dramatic colours."

FIREPLACE MANTLE Poor Jeremy. He had just finished one job and now Ellie had him making a fireplace mantel at the end of the dining room area to add some interest there and fill a bare wall. That was Renée's cue to stir up some mischief. She told Jeremy that Graeme Kelly, working with the Somervilles at Wayne and Grace's house, was also building a faux fireplace. "Well," said Jeremy, "Graeme is a fantastic carpenter but I think I've got just a little bit more creativity." "Hmm," said Renée, "the battle of the fireplaces. I think I'm going to keep my eye on these guys."

HOW TO PAINT SMOOSHING TECHNIQUE

1

glaze

two colours of paint, a light base colour and a darker top colour

several large plastic sheets
(we recommend buying an industrial roll from your local home and hardware store.)

drop cloths, paint tray, roller, brush, and items for clean-up

2

Paint base coat onto walls. Let dry.

Mix one-part paint with two-to six-parts glaze. (The more glaze you add, the more you slow down the drying time. For more opaque coverage, reduce the amount of glaze that you use.)

3

Apply glaze and paint mix over dry base coat, using a roller. Work in sections. Vary the pressure as you paint on the mixture. Press the plastic sheet to the wall, starting at the bottom and working your way up to the ceiling. Smooth plastic on, but leave enough room to play with texture and to create wrinkles.

Peel back plastic strip. If the effect on the wall is not to your liking, you may use a plastic bag to change the texture. As long as the glaze mixture is wet, it's okay to keep working. But don't let any edges dry before you start working on the next section.

4

Move on to the second section. Work as for first section, but remember to slightly overlap the previous section's wet edge. (You may use the plastic sheet that you just removed or use a new one, depending on how saturated it is with paint.) Repeat the process until the entire wall surface is covered.

DAY 2

BEADING LAMP Before she could add further fuel to this rivalry, Ellie asked Renée to apply beading to a lamp she had bought. "It's quite finicky trying to get this glue on these beads," said Renée. "Why are we doing this?" she asked. "This is a good craft for people who have patience," said Ellie. "I actually saw a lamp similar to this for about $300, compared to the $30 it's going to cost us. We're going to put a fringe around the lampshade as well. It will look quite lovely when it's done." (See how-to box.) "Maybe I don't have enough patience," mumbled Renée as she took aim again with the glue gun.

WINDOW TREATMENT Inside, Grace was enjoying a moment to herself as she transformed a green leaf-patterned fabric into window treatments with a triangular-shaped hem ending in a tassel. While Grace worked at the sewing machine, Wayne put the base coat on an unfinished blanket box that could store children's toys and also be used as a coffee table.

FINISHING TOUCHES Meanwhile, Ellie was applying burnt umber stain to a window box that would be filled with plants and separate the living room and foyer area, providing some privacy. Her final decorative touch was to hang a collage of mirrors, all shapes and sizes, along one of the walls, creating an interesting focal detail and making the room look wider than it actually is.

HOW TO **BEADED LAMP**

1

lamp with a fairly narrow base

plain white lampshade

bathtub chain — enough to wrap tightly around the entire base as well as to trim the shade

hot glue gun

fringe to edge the shade

wire cutter

2

Heat the glue gun and, starting from the bottom, start to wrap the chain tightly around the lamp base, gluing as you go. Try not to add too much glue because you want a clean, finished look and any excess glue will mark the chain.

Continue wrapping and gluing the chain, trying to maintain a consistent pattern.

3

Once you've wrapped the chain to the top of the lamp base, cut the excess and finish with a larger dab of glue.

For the shade, hot-glue the fringe along the bottom edge.

Finish by gluing a single strand of chain just above the edge of the fringe.

4

THE RESULT Once the work was completed, Ellie reviewed the space. "You have green fingernails," said Renée, "but the room looks great." "We did a smooshing job," said Ellie. "My best buys were the mirrors, bought for $5 to $80, and a wonderful antique table for $300. I'm a tad over budget," she admitted. "I owe you lunch."

BUDGET

Table (second hand)	$300.00	Houseplants	$39.06
Mirrors	$150.00	Silk Tree	$34.49
Fabric	$147.29	Sewing Supplies	$5.61
Toy Box	$129.36	Bead Trim	$5.28
Lamp	$100.00	Carpenter's Expenses	$48.93
Planter Box	$100.00		

TOTAL (EXCLUDING PAINT) **$1060.02**

AFTER TRULY CHARMING

THE CHALLENGE A bare white room that screamed, "Decorate me!" but a budget of only $1,000 to do the job. Since Wayne and Grace Price moved into their new home the living room had been sitting empty except for a piano, gate leg table and some accessories. The room was a walk-through space, opening onto the entry hall, kitchen and staircase, rather than an inviting living place.

ENGLISH COUNTRY

THE GOAL To make a usable room where Wayne and Grace can relax and entertain.

THE TEAM Neighbours Margot and Mark Sommerville, with designer Christine Newell and carpenter Graeme Kelly.

LIVING ROOM

THE SOLUTION "A blank white canvas doesn't offer much inspiration," said Christine. "So I focused on the two pieces of furniture, especially the piano as it was such a prominent piece. Since Grace and Wayne also like reading, I was immediately drawn to an English country style. Letting my imagination go, I envisioned a fireplace with bookcases on either side, two wingback chairs resting in front of the fire, a side table with glass decanters and the homeowners out on a hunt."

BEFORE **DULL BLANK WHITE WALLS**   AFTER **ENGLISH COUNTRY...IN STYLE**

DAY 1

HUNTING That last thought may have been stretching things, but it gave Christine the notion to go out hunting for bargains. She found three matching mantelpieces at a local building recovery/ re-use store and gave them to Graeme to build a fireplace, which would anchor the space and provide an architectural focal point.

WALLS Then Margot, Mark and Christine began preparing the room for painting. Since Wayne and Grace prefer neutral colours, Christine selected CIL Dulux latex eggshell Contemporary White (20YY 66/066) as the base coat. They would then do a colour wash with Stonehenge Shadow (90 YR 41/073) and Taupewood (90YR 34/084). These colours were repeated in the chintz fabric that Margot would be using to make Roman blinds, the kind that draw up into horizontal folds. "I will attempt to make Roman blinds," Margot hedged. (See how-to box, page 25.)

MANTELPIECE Outside, Graeme was chopping wood for the fireplace — mantel, that is. Once the three pieces were put together, he added a rectangular facing on the inside to give it more depth, filled in any cracks, then sanded it and primed it for painting. (See how-to box.) Renée was in a mischievous mood. "Hey Graeme is the coast clear? At the Somervilles' place they're making a faux fireplace just like you guys." "I can build a better fireplace than Jeremy (carpenter Jeremy Plant)," Graeme said. "But Renée, do me a favour and just go over there and check it out for me." Margot began to tackle the challenge of making Roman blinds while Graeme sized the fireplace frame and nailed it into place.

SPECIAL TOUCHES While all this was going on, Mark was sanding off the old green paint from a vintage side table. That done, he volunteered to help Graeme assemble the bookshelves and place them on either side of the fireplace. The room was beginning to take shape.

HOW TO **FIREPLACE MANTEL**

1

3 sheets of ³/₄-inch MDF — each ripped lengthwise into 4 pieces

mitre saw

hammer and nails

carpenter's glue

router

clamps

wood filler

metal L-brackets and screws

metal straight brackets and screws

sandpaper

paint brushes and paint (see p. 17 for technique)

2

Using the ripped pieces of MDF, make three, three-sided boxes. Make sure that the side pieces abut behind the facing piece.

Glue, nail and clamp the boxes together and let dry.

Rout each of the edges with a round over-bit.

3

FRAME

To make the mitres for the side pieces, stand them upright beside each other on a level surface. On the outside of each side pillar, mark the height and then mark a mitre at a 45-degree angle down across that face of the pillar.

Cut the mitres with the mitre saw.

4

For the top piece — decide on the width you want for the fireplace. Measure and mitre each end of the top piece to fit onto the sides. Make sure that mitres are cut across the face of the third pillar so that when the frame is done there is a hard surface around the inside of the fireplace.

Glue, nail and clamp the pieces together.

Fill any holes with wood filler. Let dry and then sand.

5

Secure the fireplace further by adding metal strips across the inside flat joints and L-brackets on the inside corner joints.

PAINT

Paint according to the instructions from page 17.

AFTER MANTELPIECE

DAY 2

SHELVING Everyone was hard at work. Margot used a glue gun to finish a valance for one of the blinds. Graeme was putting crown molding on the top of the bookshelves. "Always face your shelving in more formal rooms," he explained. "Adding facing makes the units look finished, more built in."

WALLS Renée complimented Christine on a great ragging job on the walls. "It isn't ragging, it's a three-colour wash," said Christine. "If you do a base coat and then add two other colours, one a little darker and one a little lighter than the base, it gives the walls depth." "It looks kind of like shading," said Renée.

WALLPAPER Christine pulled her aside and took out a piece of wallpaper. "I heard that Grace is really afraid we're going to put wallpaper on her walls. Why don't you go over to the Sommervilles' home (where Grace was working on their living room) and have her think we're using this." Renée, never hesitant to stir up some trouble, went off to find Grace who immediately clued in on the joke and refused to react. Hey, play along, Grace!

BOOKSHELVES Back to work. Mark and Margot began painting the bookshelves Smoky Claret latex semi-gloss (90RR 18/139). Margot admitted that she was a little nervous about using any colour since Wayne and Grace prefer everything very neutral. "But Christine thought we needed some colour," she said. "And I really think they're going to like it."

MIRROR Renée painted cold tea onto some sheets of music to give them an aged look, while Christine showed Margot how to sponge on cream gold paint to give a gold leaf look to the corners of an antique mirror. The mirror was hung over the fireplace, two andirons set flanking the fireplace with two pale blue wing chairs, a bargain at $300 for the pair, placed in front, and a flea market coffee table nearby. The music sheets were rolled, tied with gold ribbon and put on top of the piano.

THE RESULT "Accessories always play a large part in pulling a room together," said Christine. "Finding the right accessories, glass decanters, lamps and candlesticks, completed the room. These are the touches that bring life into a space that can otherwise be a trifle impersonal."

BUDGET

Two Wingback Chairs			Small Cabinet and Ornaments	
(garage sale)	$300.00		(second hand)	$27.76
Fabric and Hardware			Fabric Lining/Tassels	
for Roman Blinds	$121.28		for Roman Blinds	$21.29
Other Garage Sale Items, Various	$63.50		Spanish Moss	$19.17
Planter Tropical Plants/			Andirons/Decanters	
Accessories	$62.90		(second hand)	$14.58
Mantels for Fireplace	$50.00		Fresh Flowers	$14.00
Crackle Glaze and Paint			Spray Paint/Varnish	$12.64
for Fireplace/Walls	$43.55		Cabinet Handles/Lamp Parts	$7.54
			Carpenter's Expenses	$118.12
			TOTAL (EXCLUDING PAINT)	**$876.33**

HOW TO EASY ROMAN BLINDS

1

a

THESE ROMAN BLINDS ARE NOT THE TRADITIONAL ONES. THEY ARE MADE TO FIT INSIDE THE WINDOW FRAME AND GIVE A MUCH MORE LOOSE AND FREE-FLOWING LOOK.

fabric cut to measure the window as follows: width + 2 inches x inside sill height + 12 inches

fabric tape

1 1-inch x 4-inch board — cut to fit inside width of window

plastic rings for Roman blinds

small metal eye hooks

nylon cording (plenty!)

sewing machine and thread

staple gun and staples

needle and thread

hammer and nails

3

Sew a 1-inch hem around the entire piece of fabric.

On the back of the fabric, press a strip of tape running the whole length of the fabric 2 ½ inches in from each side. You should have a strip of tape on each side of the fabric.

Place strips across the rest of the fabric, making sure they are equidistant. (We placed ours every 11 inches.)

At the top and bottom, fold the 1-inch hem under and sew another hem 2 ½ inches wide.

4

Starting 2 inches from the edge of the top hem, hand-sew the plastic rings onto the middle of the fabric tape at 8- to 10-inch intervals. The last ring should be right next to the top of the bottom hem.

Repeat by sewing plastic rings onto the other horizontal tape strips, making sure all of the rings are aligned horizontally.

5

Place the 1-inch x 4-inch board so that its lower edge lines up with the lower edge of the upper hem on the fabric. Holding the fabric in place, flip the board over and staple the fabric to the board on the 4-inch side.

Holding the board on the bad side of the fabric, line the eye hooks up with the rows of plastic rings. Screw the hooks into the board in a row about ½ an inch from the inside edge. Insert another, slightly larger, eye hook on the far left side of the board.

Starting on the right side, tie cording to the bottom plastic ring and run it vertically through the rest of the rings, including the eye hook. Repeat for each row of plastic rings and eye hooks.

Run the cords through the large eye hook on the far left of the board — leave about 18 inches of cord hanging. Once all the cords are attached, tie the overhang sections together.

Nail the board to the inside of the upper sill. Pull overhang cords on the left to raise and lower the blind.

THE CHALLENGE The living/dining room in Julie and Pete Bozanis' house is long and narrow with a triangular niche at one end flanked by two tall windows. Julie and Pete had bought new furniture, put in new hardwood floors and painted the room neutral pale green. The result was an uninteresting space, plain with no personality. Pete was open to changes as long as they didn't include his new floor. Julie said she had heard that shag rugs are back in. "We're not too enthusiastic about that," she said. "And we don't like animal prints — no tiger stripes or leopard spots."

A BY THE BOOK

THE GOAL To create a room Julie and Pete can use for entertaining. Since the couple are both teachers, designer Oreet Fagan decided she would begin with a book theme.

THE TEAM Julie's sister-in-law Dawn Ullman and Dawn's father-in-law Ron Ullman, with designer Oreet Fagan and carpenter Michael Ash.

LIVING ROOM

THE SOLUTION Oreet's first impression of the room was that it had no focal point. Then there was the irregular-shaped niche at one end. It was not large enough to use as a conversation area containing two chairs, but it was too large to simply ignore. Oreet selected colours — a moss green, CIL Dulux Caisson Green flat latex (45 YY 24/158), to go with the existing furniture, and a hot red, Salsa low lustre satin latex (10 YR 14/348) for a feature wall and accents. White Mountain semi-gloss latex (50 DD 83/020) would be used for trim. She found striped fabric in red, white, olive and burnished gold that she would use for window treatments and throw cushions.

BEFORE LONG AND NARROW, WITH MISPLACED FURNITURE   AFTER A FUNCTIONAL AND DRAMATIC ROOM

DAY 1

WALLS Dawn and Ron began by taping a diamond pattern on two of the walls while Oreet was rolling a coat of red onto the back wall. Whoops, Oreet, that's an awfully bright red. Are you sure you know what you're doing?

LAMPS The taping completed, Ron got rolling with the Caisson Green paint while Dawn saw the light — three lights to be exact. Oreet showed her how to make a unique craft project, creating red cone-shaped hanging lamps. "This is the coolest lamp," said Dawn. "I'm using a template to cut out a pattern from this red fabric and the rest is a matter of gluing things together and adding a tassel. Each lamp costs just $10."

SHELVES Michael built a long, low shelf, which would hold the large TV and provide storage for the VCR and videotapes. He then hung a mantel overtop of the set. Oreet's plan was to make the TV resemble the shape of a fireplace, set against the red wall.

WALL TEXTURE Back to the green walls where everything was still rolling along. Oreet showed Ron how to paint every second diamond with a coat of water-based high gloss Varathane, giving the wall a subtle texture. Renée approved, "You know what they say — diamonds are a girl's best friend."

TABLES Outside, Michael finished an irregular-shaped desk to fit in the window niche. Ron painted the TV table with eggshell latex black Dark Secret (00NN 05/000) while Renée chose the Salsa red to paint the corner desktop. Oreet painted a black stovepipe design in the middle of the bright red walls to complete the faux fireplace look. "This feature wall will draw your eye to the far end of the room," Oreet explained.

HOW TO BOOK END TABLE

THIS IS A TWO-PART PROJECT, BUILDING THE TABLE BOX (THIS PAGE) AND APPLYING THE BOOK BINDINGS (NEXT PAGE).

BOX

1/2 sheet of 3/4-inch MDF	100 grit (or finer) sandpaper
4 1/4-inch X 3/4-inch X 36-inch strips balsawood	carpenter's glue
table saw	masking tape
hammer	1 1/2-inch finishing nails
drill with 1/16-inch bit	wood filler

1  Using a table saw, cut MDF into 2 end pieces measuring 16 inches x 14 inches. Cut another piece of MDF into 2 side pieces measuring 16 inches x 20 inches. Finally, cut MDF top and bottom pieces measuring 15 3/4 inches x 20 1/2 inches. Along each edge on the top and bottom pieces, cut out a rabbet 1 inch wide x 1/2 inch deep so that all edges have a lip 1 inch wide x 1/4 inch thick.

Cut a channel 1/8 inch deep x 1/4 inch wide down the middle of the balsawood strips.

2 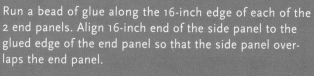 Cut four 4-inch square blocks from scraps of MDF for feet.

Pre-drill 1/16-inch holes through the face of each side panel (16 inches x 20 inches) every 4 inches around the perimeter. Set the drilled holes 3/8 inch in from the edges.

Run a bead of glue along the 16-inch edge of each of the 2 end panels. Align 16-inch end of the side panel to the glued edge of the end panel so that the side panel overlaps the end panel.

3 Using a hammer, gently insert the finishing nails into the pre-drilled holes and nail the pieces together. Repeat this process until you have made a box that measures 15 1/2 inches deep x 20 inches wide x 16 inches high.

Insert the top and bottom pieces in a similar manner, ensuring that both pieces have a 1/4-inch overlap on 3 faces of the box. This overlap simulates the outer binding of the books.

Set all nails, fill, let dry and sand.

Divide the space along the front and back ends horizontally into three equal sections and draw dividing lines.

Over the lines, centre strips of balsawood onto 3 sides with the channel side facing out. Glue into position and hold secure with masking tape until dry.

Paint box feet black. Let dry. Glue onto the base with carpenter's glue.

(CONTINUED NEXT PAGE)

HOW TO **BOOK END TABLE** (CONT)

4

5

6

BOOK BINDINGS

1 length aluminum gutter guard (cut to the width of the table front)

hot glue gun and glue

newspaper torn into strips approximately 12 inches x 2 inches

all-purpose flour mixed with water to a paste

3 different colours of paint (e.g. red, green, tan)

black latex paint (for trim)

gold craft paint (for faux pages)

burnt umber

glaze

small and medium stiff paint brushes.

Cut aluminum gutter guard into three 20 ½-inch lengths and bend or flatten curve as required so that the width across measures 5 ¼ inches.

Dip newspaper into papier mâché mixture (flour and water paste). Wipe off excess. Apply to gutter guard. Continue process until entire guard is covered Repeat with remaining guards, and let them dry thoroughly.

Once dry, glue the guards to the table front between pieces of balsa trim. Let dry.

Paint the trim in black — to demarcate the "books."

Paint each of the gutter guards a different colour. This will create the "spines" of the "books." Don't forget to paint the top of the table the same colour as the top book spine.

Mix a flat gold craft paint with a few drops of burnt umber and glaze (1 part paint to 5 parts glaze). Using a stiff brush, drag mixture across the sides and back of the table, to create "pages."

You may finish the look by applying a book title stencil (or handpainted title) to the top of the table.

AFTER A PLACE FOR CONVERSATION AND READING

DAY 2

BOOK END TABLE Dawn was happily noting novel design tricks. "There are some great ideas I'd like to take from here to adapt to my place," she said. One of them certainly was the end table that Ron and Michael were putting together. First they built a box, 15 ½ inches deep by 20 inches wide and 16 inches high, with a ¼-inch overlap on one side (three faces) of the box. Ron painted the table legs black then glued them into place. Michael added some trim. Then Oreet showed Ron how to apply a papier mâché mixture of flour and water paste to create the illusion of book spines. (See how-to box.) The finished table looks like three large books stacked one on top of the other, a definite conversation piece and perfect for the room's overall book theme.

PILLOWS But all was not meant to be scholarly and serious as Renée discovered when Oreet asked her to make a pillow using a child's soccer ball wrapped in fabric batting. The ball was covered with a long cover of red fabric that was closed with elastic bands at both ends around the soccer ball and then tied with Oreet's striped fabric to become a candy wrapper pillow. Renée surveyed her finished project and announced, "Well, I'm having a ball."

FINISHING TOUCHES A large overstuffed chair was placed in one corner with Dawn's red hanging lights, each with a chandelier light bulb, glowing overhead. The bookcase was moved near the new built-in window niche desk, striped throw pillows and the candy pillow were tossed onto the couch. And the room was ready for viewing.

THE RESULT "This room used to be subtle, now it's dramatic," said Renée. "Isn't it awesome!" said Dawn. Julie and Pete agreed.

BUDGET

Bookcase	$105.93	Bowl	$32.09
Framed Pictures (3)	$80.22	Black Shelf	$32.04
Area Rug	$74.85	Bookends	$27.80
Fabric and Thread	$58.31	Picture Matting	$26.74
Light Fixture	$42.75	Clock	$21.39
Silk Flowers	$40.12	Screws, Hinge, Mesh	$20.30
Twigs, Craft Supplies	$41.06	Silk Plants	$13.90
Faux Greenery	$37.10	Wicker Basket	$10.69
Hardware Supplies	$36.27	Carpenter's Expenses	$89.13
Glass Vase	$32.10		

TOTAL (EXCLUDING PAINT)   **$822.79**

THE CHALLENGE Jenny and John Kapralos are a young couple who enjoy entertaining, but they weren't happy with the ambiance of their living room and the dining room that opened onto it. They had tried decorating on their own, but the rooms didn't turn out the way they had envisioned. The space was too traditional and conservative, not contemporary and comfortable. After their baby arrived, there just wasn't time to start decorating again.

CONTEMPORARY

THE GOAL A living room and dining room that would better reflect the Kapralos' style, contemporary and hip, rather than old-fashioned. The rooms would also have to be easy to keep tidy because of the couple's young child.

THE TEAM John's younger sister Voula and his mother Anna, along with designer Michael Vuxsta and carpenter Jeremy Plant.

LIVING

THE SOLUTION Michael knew he would have to work around the furniture that was already in place, primarily large sofas and the dining room set. He wanted to give the rooms some Greek elements, since he knew that Jenny and John liked that influence.

BEFORE **A ROOM WITH NO SENSE OF ORDER**   AFTER **NOW IT'S RICH, SLEEK AND URBANE**

DAY 1

WALLS The first step was repainting the walls that had been painted a gold tone with a faux finish. Michael chose to separate the spaces and open up each room by painting with a flat latex. For the living room he chose CIL Dulux Stowe White (45YY 83/062) and for the dining room, taupe, Bramble Tan (10YY 48/071). Both colours would provide the background for a modern, minimal look. Top priority was teaching Voula, who had a lot of enthusiasm but no previous experience, how to paint walls. She proved to be an eager learner and soon settled into a steady rhythm of brush strokes and occasional spills.

FOCAL POINT Michael decided to concentrate on the living room since the dining room was dominated by the table and chairs. And because the living room has good basics — hardwood floors, a new window — nothing horrible that had to be ripped out, the renovation would be more cosmetic than construction. He determined that the fireplace should be the room's focal point and asked Jeremy to build a wooden cap for the mantel.

TABLES & CHAIRS Jeremy would also be responsible for building living room tables, a side table and a coffee table that Michael designed. But the room would be left uncluttered, open enough that Jenny and John could add to it later. Michael said he wanted to provide a good canvas and let them contribute their own personal touches.

UPHOSTERY While Jeremy worked on the living room table, carefully measuring then cutting and assembling pieces, Voula graduated from painting to upholstery as Michael showed her some stapling tricks. She started to recover the dining room chairs with a white fabric squared with fine charcoal gray lines.

SPECIAL TOUCHES Time to introduce a subtle Greek influence in the form of a serving tray made by Anna with instructions from Michael. He started with a black rectangular picture frame that he bought for $2 and added a photocopied Greek scene to make a lovely decorative touch. Anna's job was to put them together. (See how-to box.) Michael added another picture-perfect touch by framing copies of photos of Greece from his own collection. The black and white pictures are dramatic, set on white matting with black wooden frames.

HOW TO PICTURE FRAME SERVING TRAY

1

rectangular, wooden picture frame

picture or photograph (to go inside the picture frame)

dark-coloured felt

white school glue

2 drawer handles

2

Place picture in frame.

Attach handles to front sides of frame.

Cut felt for the back of the frame to size.

Use school glue to attach felt to back of frame. Let dry.

3

4

BEFORE **LIGHT AND AIRY WITH PLEASING STRAIGHT LINES**

DAY 2

FINAL FABRIC Voula was finishing the last of the dining room chair covers. Anna was busy ironing new curtains while Michael freshened a lamp shade with some white spray paint.

LIGHTING Jeremy built a square lamp base and fastened the legs to the coffee table. Then he and Michael did some pocket cutting, carefully lifting out the centre of the wood frame to serve as the base for the glass tabletop. Voula was ready for another lesson in painting, this time to spray paint the coffee table legs and top in a silver gray.

FINISHING TOUCHES Finally, a framed mirror, matching the mahogany-stained fireplace cap, was hung over the mantel. A silver clock and silver vase were arranged as accessories.

THE RESULT Michael said his biggest challenge was getting Voula to paint the wall correctly. But he was pleased with the result. His best buys for old items were auction finds: the silver clock for $10 and the vase for $12. His best new buys were the curtain panels for $20 and the lamp for $33. Who knew there could be so much luxury for so little? "Basically, everything was a good buy," he said. "And there's enough left over for a bottle of wine."

BUDGET

Wicker Chest	$175.00	Silver Accessories	$38.04
Mirror	$105.00	Fabric for Chair	$33.32
Coffee Table Glass	$90.67	Pillows	$32.00
Curtain Rods	$70.00	Lamps	$30.00
Curtain Panels	$60.00	Desk Lamp	$20.13
Jute Rug	$57.47	Carpenter's Expenses	$242.10
		TOTAL (EXCLUDING PAINT)	**$953.73**

AFTER A COOL CONTEMPORARY LOOK

THE CHALLENGE Dawn and Brett Ullman's kitchen had been renovated by the previous owners in a country theme that just didn't suit the Ullmans' taste. Dawn and Brett had already redone most of the rest of the house and wanted their kitchen to fit in, but they didn't know how to begin. Since there was no dining room, the breakfast area would have to be stylish enough to serve a dual purpose. "I want something that is contemporary and classy," Dawn said.

A SANTA FE-STYLE

THE GOAL Create a room that will fit in with the rest of the house, a room that will have clean lines, contemporary style and definite flair.

THE TEAM Brett's sister Julie and her husband Pete, along with designer Tracy Kundell and carpenter Graeme Kelly.

KITCHEN

THE SOLUTION First of all, Tracy wanted to get rid of the country dot print wallpaper and border. And so the team started on a tear, stripping the wallpaper and preparing the wall for further treatment. Then Pete helped Graeme take out the old kitchen countertop, which was dark emerald green, accentuating the smallness of the actual workspace. By also removing a breakfast bar, they opened up the dining area and made the room more spacious.

BEFORE **OUTDATED COUNTRY DOT WALLPAPER AND BORDER**   AFTER **A SANTE FE-STYLE KITCHEN THAT REALLY COOKS**

DAY 1

WALLS Tracy had selected colours for the kitchen inspired by a painting with reddish rust tones in an adjoining room. She also found some perfect peel-and-stick floor tiles, resembling green slate, at the hardware store. Since other rooms on the first floor were green, green would be the base colour.

FLOOR The natural appearance of the "slate" floor tiles also inspired the wall treatment, a Santa Fe adobe textured look, using a paper pulp product, Textureline Adobe Strippable Plaster. Once the plaster was tinted with CIL Dulux Country Cream eggshell latex (4044 76/112), Julie was put to work using a trowel to apply it and then a string roller to give the walls a stippled effect. Since the process has a long drying period, Julie had time to work with the texture. The walls were left to harden overnight before more colour was added. (See how-to box.)

KITCHEN COUNTER Renée got a quick lesson from Graeme on how to cut a base for the kitchen counter. Then Graeme was ready to apply parchment cream colour laminate, another hardware store find, to the counter. He cut the laminate sheeting allowing about a half-inch overhang. Once the top was in place he applied contact cement. "Careful," warned Renée, "once it sticks down, it's stuck down." Once the countertop was securely in place, Graeme trimmed off the excess laminate with a router. He then used wood edging for a finished look.

SPECIAL TOUCHES Meanwhile, Pete was giving a pewter finish to the pine kitchen dining set that combined natural wood tabletop and chair seats with legs and chairbacks painted green. Pete sanded and primed all the green painted areas, then painted them silver using Textureline metal paint. Later, he used a dry brush with black latex paint to enhance the pewter look. (See how-to box, page 42.)

BACKSPLASH Over at the counter space, Tracy and Julie were preparing sand-coloured tiles for the backsplash. Tracy had asked the hardware store to precut all the tile pieces. Getting your tiles precut saves on buying or renting special equipment. Tracy had already designed a pattern, using subway tiles in combination with diamond shaped tiles, so it was just a matter of fitting the tiles on the wall with tile adhesive and a serrated-edge spatula, allowing enough space between each tile for grout. Even unfinished, the back-splash added flair to the room.

HOW TO SANTA FE ADOBE WALL TREATMENT

1

Textureline Adobe Strippable Plaster
roller with a string roller sleeve
plastic knock-down blade
large metal trowel or spatula
Textureline Zero Gloss Varnish

2

Prepare and prime all walls and let dry completely.

To make the adobe finish strippable, cover the wall entirely with wallpaper sizing. Let dry.

Working in approximately 4-foot x 4-foot sections, trowel on the adobe plaster.

3

Roll the string roller through the plaster in single swipes. This will produce a stippled effect. Lightly run the plastic knock-down blade over the rolled surface, knocking down the stippled surface but leaving subtle ridges and valleys. (This product has an open time of 6 hours so if you make a mistake just re-trowel and start again.)

Continue this process for the rest of the wall surfaces and let dry overnight.

4

Once the walls are dry, finish with a paint colour or wash of your choice.

When paint is dry, seal all the surfaces with a coat of Textureline's Zero Gloss Varnish.

5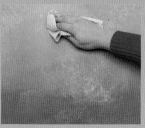

SPECIAL THANKS TO TEXTURELINE'S DECORATIVE ARTIST BARRY AFFLECK
FOR THE PHOTOS OF THIS PROJECT

DAY 2

KITCHEN COUNTER First on the agenda was setting the new counter in place. The men worked together to lay it down carefully and it really looked good. Graeme cut a hole for the sink. "Be careful," Renée was supervising, "you've only got one chance. You'd better not mess this up." "She never trusts me," said Graeme.

WALLS Tracy and Julie were giving a colour wash to the walls with Shenadoah Valley (50GY 41/084), an earthy green, dry brushed on very lightly to maintain the adobe texture. Renée was enlisted to help, dabbing with a damp sponge to blend in the colour after Julie applied the green paint. Then Tracy painted Pompeii Clay (60YR 33/287) a brown tone on top of the green. After that, Tracy applied Textureline silver metal paint highlights and then the walls were sealed with a coat of varnish.

PEWTERING With the walls completed, Julie took over the pewtering role, turning two gold-coloured light fixtures that Tracy had bought into silvered chandeliers. Pete continued this silver theme, replacing all the wooden knobs on the cupboards with chrome-coloured handles. Then he and Renée peeled, stuck and rolled out a new floor using the slate look-alike tiles, laying them on a diagonal grid to make the room appear larger. Meanwhile, it was time for Tracy to grout the backsplash tiles, using a matching sand-coloured grout applied with a spatula, and quickly wiping off excess grout before it dried.

SPECIAL TOUCHES The final touch was installing lighting under the cabinets. When the lights were turned on, they added real ambiance to a room already high on the "wow factor" rating.

HOW TO EASY PEWTER FINISH

piece to be finished — we used a cheap gilt frame

fine grit sand paper

small paint brush with tray

artist's brush

Textureline silver latex paint

soft cloth

1 tube of black Rub & Buff, or any black acrylic artist's paint with a gel-like consistency

Give the piece a light sanding and then clean it with water and TSP.

Paint one or two coats of the metallic silver paint. Let dry.

Once dry, take the Rub & Buff, or acrylic paint, and dab a small amount on the corner of a soft rag or dry paint brush.

Working in one direction, start to rub or brush the black acrylic over the silver paint so that there is a transparent layer over the silver.

As you continue, make sure that you let the a little more black seep into the cracks or imperfections — this will give you a more authentic finish.

Let dry.

BEFORE & AFTER **FROM A BASIC BUILDER'S KITCHEN TO THE WARMTH OF SANTA FE**

THE RESULT "Kitchens require a lot of detail work," said Tracy. "My best buys were labour — Graeme did a great job with the countertop and Julie and I did a good job with the backsplash. The knobs were left over from another job I had done so they didn't cost anything, and we got the look of slate for the floor for only $1.60 a square foot."

"This kitchen looked unconnected and bland. We warmed it up to create a unified look," Renée enthused.

BUDGET

Tiles and Grout	$316.95	Drapery Hardware	$106.87
Light Fixtures and Bulbs	$132.63	Picture	$101.65
Drapery Fabric	$121.25	Cupboard Hardware	$23.70
Counter Top	$108.11		
		TOTAL (EXCLUDING PAINT)	**$911.16**

THE CHALLENGE Catherine and Brian Wilson's kitchen was outdated, stuck in the 1970s with dark wooden cupboards and countertops in poor condition. This is a room that is used a lot and as a consequence it appeared much the worse for wear. Catherine said the room needed a lift. "And I'd love to see the cupboards refinished." Brian added that he was pretty much open to anything. "I'm not handy and Ernest (see team members) is handy so I think we're getting the better end of this."

A FRENCH COUNTRY

THE GOAL To brighten the kitchen, eliminate some clutter and add sizzle to a space that had been left on the back burner too long.

THE TEAM Catherine's co-worker Hennie and her husband Ernest Price, along with designer Christine Newell and carpenter Bill Crossman.

KITCHEN

THE SOLUTION Christine found her inspiration when she walked into the kitchen and saw a closet at one end with huge floor-to-ceiling tin doors. The closet was definitely uninspiring but its dimensions and framework gave her ideas. "With a little bit of construction, we could make a beautiful built-in country dresser — perfect for a French Country look." That look would include yellow, washed walls, with copper pots and utensils hanging from a pot rack and a French Provençal sunny yellow and warm blue colour scheme. Okay team, prepare for takeoff to southeast France!

THE INSPIRATION **FLOOR TO CEILING CLOSET**   BEFORE & AFTER **THESE CUPBOARDS NEEDED A LIFT SO WE TOOK THEM TO THE FRENCH COUNTRY**

DAY 1

CUPBOARDS The first step was to remove all the kitchen cupboard doors and counter drawers so they could be sanded, painted with an undercoat and then a white latex semi-gloss, CIL Dulux White Mountain (50BB 83/020). While this was going on, carpenter Bill started working on the new kitchen counter. Since the area near the sink had rotted, he decided to put down a new plywood top. Bill's such a cutup he even included a hole for the kitchen sink.

WALLS Once this carpentry was done, Ernest could finish the base coat for the walls. The walls and ceiling would be painted yellow, CIL Dulux latex eggshell Coneflower (20YY 61/331) for the walls and a softer shade, Lis Creme (30 YY 77/169), for the ceiling.

KITCHEN COUNTER The peninsula counter was a problem since it was higher than the rest of the counter surface. Bill said, no problem, and built a new one. Then he finished it and the rest of the countertop with neat, yellow ceramic tiles. (See how-to box.)

SPECIAL TOUCHES Meanwhile, Christine was turning the panel from an old door into a chalkboard, priming it, applying a faux finish for the frame and then applying a special blackboard paint. "How handy for a kitchen," Renée said as she stopped by to check on the progress and offer some help.

BEFORE & AFTER LOWERING THE COUNTERTOP AND ADDING NEW TILES GIVES THE ROOM MORE WARMTH

HOW TO TILING COUNTERTOPS

tiles	tile float	wooden stir stick
grout	small piece of wooden dowel	sponge
bucket for mixing grout		tile cutter
bucket for cleaning tile	tile adhesive	measuring tape
notched trowel	level	

 **1**

The surface for tiling should be flat and protected against water damage — check with your local hardware store for tips and products.

Dry-fit the tiles, using the tile cutter to help fit the edges.

Once the tile has been dry-fitted, number and remove.

 **2**

Working in sections, use the slotted trowel to apply a good layer of the tile adhesive to the tiling surface.

Immediately place the tile, using a level to ensure the tiles are straight.

Continue until all the tiles are in place and let dry over night.

 **3**

Once dry, mix the grout according to the package directions.

Place the grout on the surface and use the tile float to force the grout into all spaces between the tiles. Sponge off any excess grout.

 **4**

Once most of the grout has been removed from the tile surfaces, clean up the grout lines using the rounded edge of the small piece of doweling.

Once dry, clean and polish the surface with a clean rag.

DAY 2

FRENCH DRESSER Bill started the French dresser, building a valance top over three open shelves with a closed cupboard at the bottom. Christine was actually quite pleased to find that the inside walls of the closet were in rough shape. "This was great because the distressed look on the inside of the dresser adds rather than distracts from the country look we were going for. It's as if generations of people had been using this cabinet."

HOW TO THREE-COLOUR WALL WASH

paint roller and tray

bucket

water

paint mixing stick

sponge or rags

gloves

base coat paint colour

two complementary paint colours

Apply the base coat. Let it dry completely. (Approximately 2 hours for latex paints.)

Mix one part of your first complementary paint colour to one part glaze and one part water. (Remember that the colour you apply last will be the most dominant.) Stir mixture.

Dip a sponge or rag into the paint mixture and squeeze out excess.

"Wash" colour onto the walls using a circular motion. Work in sections no larger than 3 feet x 3 feet. Keep in mind that less rubbing will give a more distressed look to your walls.

Let first application of colour dry. Mix one-part of your second paint colour to one part glaze and one part water. Stir. "Wash" colour onto walls using a circular motion. Let dry. Enjoy your new look!

FINISHING TOUCHES Adding to this patina, Christine and Hennie chose to colour wash the walls in three tones over the yellow base coat to give a sun-drenched look. (See how-to box.) Brian was finishing the white cupboard doors and drawers, replacing the handles.

A garage sale find window was framed by shutters painted CIL Dulux Falling Star (37YY 78/312), a latex eggshell in cornflower blue. Hennie sewed up some Roman blinds for the windows using fabric with yellow fruits scattered over a deep blue background. The final touches included a decoupage of fruits on an unfinished wooden tray and a pot rack hung from the ceiling, accessorized with garage sale copper pots and dried herbs tied in bunches.

THE RESULT Catherine and Brian had smiles as sunny as their new kitchen when they viewed the amazing transformation. Christine advises to not be afraid to use colour. She says that when you have a small budget, the accessories that you add to a room can provide the biggest impact.

AFTER **FRENCH CLOSET WITH VALANCE AND COLOUR-WASHED WALLS**

BUDGET

Tiles, Grout	$169.00	Tulip Tea Lights		$18.40
Fabric for Roman Blinds	$129.83	Copper Utensils (second hand)		$14.47
Kitchen Faucets	$85.53	Door Handles		$12.53
Pot Rack	$75.90	Chalkboard Door, Glass Door		$11.90
Plants, Plant Holders	$57.21	Decoupage		$10.93
Craft Supplies	$52.84	Lasagna Dish with Basket		$10.35
Ceramic Cupboard Fixtures	$41.02	China Chicken		$8.04
Lining, Cord and Rings for Blinds	$18.68	Carpenter's Expenses		$253.12
		TOTAL (EXCLUDING PAINT)		**$969.75**

THE CHALLENGE Kate Stewart and Bret Dawson had been living in their house for four years. While they had done some painting in other rooms, they couldn't decide what to do with the beige colonial kitchen with its grungy-looking wooden kitchen cupboards. "I've changed some light bulbs, Kate's been to the hardware store a couple of times. We're singularly unprepared for this," said Bret. "We're not handy people." "We're looking for some modern elements, some cleaner lines," Kate explained. "We're not afraid of colour. We want to stay away from the country bumpkin look," she added. "We're not into the whole white picket fence thing."

COLONIAL TO INDUSTRIAL

THE GOAL To modernize the kitchen, eliminate the drab beige colonial and give it a sleek, industrial look.

THE TEAM Kate and Bret's friends, Shelley White and Sean Stanleigh, with designer Karen Adler and carpenter Michael Ash.

KITCHEN

THE SOLUTION Karen decided immediately that a radical makeover was in order since the house had been bought from the original owner who had not renovated. She began by calling the gas company to move the gas lines so that appliances could be shifted to another wall where they wouldn't be as visible.

AFTER **AN INDUSTRIAL UPDATE**   AFTER **THE FINISHED CABINET**

DAY 1

WALLS While Sean and Michael started unhinging cabinet doors and removing drawers, numbering each one to note where it had come from, Karen and Shelley tore off the old wallpaper border under the ceiling, preparing to paint the walls in grape and gold latex eggshell. "Bold colours for a kitchen," Renée remarked. "They're very bold people," Shelley said, as she started with CIL Dulux Gothic Grape (50RB 18/149). Karen's notion was to make the room look larger with colour blocking — a square of grape here, there a rectangle of CIL Dulux Moonstruck gold (2044 53/423).

CUPBOARDS Outside Michael and Karen began meshing around with the colonial cupboards, giving them a high-tech look with standard mesh aluminum screen, washers and large screws. (See how-to box.) To complete this look, the hinges were sprayed with metal paint and new knobs were attached. Karen suggested that as an inexpensive alternative to new knobs, a large bolt and screw could be used.

PAINT Since most of the original beige had been purpled over, Shelley taped out squares in readiness for painting them gold. "A paintastic day," Renée observed.

HOW TO MODERN MESH CABINETRY UPDATE

1

2

3

4

5
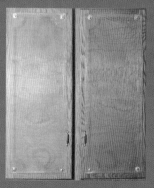

old style wooden cabinetry

aluminum mesh screening (make sure it has a slight stiffness)

silver nuts, bolts and large washers — 4 of each per cabinet.

utility knife

metal awl

metal straight edge

drill and drill bit large enough to drill a hole for the bolt

wrench

primer, metallic paint and brushes (optional)

Measure the dimensions of each cabinet then subtract an inch from each side. These will be the measurements for the mesh overlay.

To make the mesh overlay, start with the cabinet measurements then double the width and subtract ½ an inch. Cut out a piece of mesh this size.

Fold the mesh in half and flatten the fold with the metal straight edge.

To make clean edges, fold over a half-inch "hem" on each side, flattening each edge with the metal straight edge.

Line up the mesh on the cabinet door and place the washers at each corner. Mark the middle of each washer.

Remove the mesh and drill a hole.

Replace the mesh and use an awl to poke a hole where the bolts will go.

Attach the mesh with the nuts, bolts and washers.

Continue with the rest of the cabinets, then re-hang.

For a more industrial look, prime and paint all the cupboards with a silver metallic paint (optional).

DAY 2

PAINT Day Two dawned sunny, but soon turned into a nightmare morning. When the tape around the purple sections was pulled off, paint came with it. No one had thought to prime the walls, and years of grease and grime meant the paint just wouldn't stick. So it was back to the beginning for the team as they peeled off paint in pathetic, purple globs and began to prime. Sean found solace in the garden, justifying his retreat from the chaotic kitchen scene by spray painting the refrigerator door silver.

BACKSPLASH Since many hands were now making light work of the paint situation, Karen could turn her attention to the old ceramic backsplash between the cupboards and the kitchen counter. She had found some black leather placemats. (Other washable place-mats would do, she said.) They were glued to the backsplash with heavy duty adhesive, and trimmed with a craft knife (preferably at the top where cuts would be less noticeable). "They add texture, cover the old backsplash and give the kitchen a modern look," Karen said. "They're easily washable and they cost under $5 per square foot."

WINDOW TREATMENT Karen asked Shelley to help her with a window curtain, using a threaded rod and plastic mesh placemats sewn together. (See how-to box.) The finished window treatment was neat and metallic, allowing sunlight in but providing privacy as well.

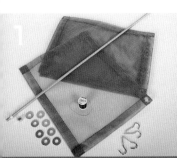 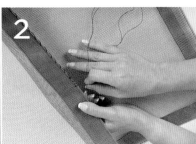  

HOW TO INDUSTRIAL WINDOW TREATMENT

metal threaded rod long enough to span the chosen window

curtain rod hardware to fit the metal threaded rod

2 large chunky bolts that will screw onto the threaded rod

10 large round silver washers with a centre hole large enough to slip over the rod

needle and silver thread

10 metallic silver mesh placemats — they should be at least 18 inches wide x 12 inches high

To make the curtain panels, line up 5 of the placemats with the longer side on the horizontal.

Carefully sew the placemats together to make one long panel.

Repeat for the second panel.

Space the washers evenly across the top of the panels — 5 on each — and attach with the needle and thread.

Install the curtain rod holders over the window.

Feed the washers onto the threaded rod.

Place the rod on the holder and finish by screwing the large bolts over each end of the threaded rod.

AFTER AN INDUSTRIAL SPACE WITH SOME GREAT PUNCHES OF COLOUR

FINISHING TOUCHES Michael built a narrow breakfast bar along one side of the room, then a large blackboard made from a panel painted with special blackboard paint was hung above the bar. Time was running out, but Sean was all wired up as he and Shelley hung a new light fixture. The final touch was a $79 patchwork rug, pulling a range of colours together and hiding the floor. A recipe was quickly chalked on the blackboard, some greenery added and this kitchen was no longer grimly colonial, but lively and cool.

THE RESULT Karen said that aside from the painting disaster, she was really pleased with the finished product. She suggested that since hardware is very expensive in a kitchen, budget-conscious renovators should use things that aren't typically meant for kitchens. "I usually start a project by walking through the hardware store, looking for inexpensive products and asking myself how can I use them."

BUDGET

Doorknobs and Shelf	$369.03	Aluminum Screen	$57.68
Placemats and Rug	$294.13	Chalkboard Paint, Primer	$25.70
Accessories	$98.32	Apples	$29.86
Hardware (screws, bolts, etc.)	$67.81		
		TOTAL (EXCLUDING PAINT)	**$942.53**

THE CHALLENGE Roger and Kim Mitchell had a large, dark bedroom. The walls were deep blue, the carpet green and there were a few pieces of furniture to fill up the space. Roger, describing himself as a man of simple pleasures, suggested that a mirror on the ceiling might be nice. However, Kim nixed that idea and said that she didn't have any special preferences except that she wouldn't like a canary yellow room. Other than that, the decorating team was free to use their skills and imagination.

A FRENCH COUNTRY

THE GOAL To brighten this bedroom space, making it feel more comfortable, despite the large area and, of course, avoiding ceiling mirrors.

THE TEAM The Mitchells' next-door neighbours, Suzanne and Andrew Marshall, with designer Michelle Petrie and carpenter Genia Fromme.

BEDROOM

THE SOLUTION Michelle said, "The room was so large and had very little in it so I knew that our $1,000 budget would be stretched to the limit (which it was — but we did it). I also knew that the existing grass green carpet would narrow the range of choice for the colour palette. Almost immediately, the colour of the carpet suggested French Country to me. Emerald green was Napoleon's favourite colour so you see a lot of it in French design."

BEFORE **BIG, BLUE AND BARE**   AFTER **OLD WORLD FRENCH FLAIR**

DAY 1

WALLS Painting the walls and ceiling was the first step. Michelle decided to neutralize the bright colour of the rug by using the opposite colour on the colour wheel. Red would reduce the intensity of the green carpet and she wanted to select a colour that would go with the bedspread she had bought and the lined ivory and green floral patterned drapes she had found at a yard sale. Since Roger was quite emphatic that he disliked pinks and yellows, Michelle chose a putty colour for the walls with pink in it, latex eggshell CIL Dulux Silk Moire (30YR64/044), that the team thereafter referred to as "stone" to avoid any reference to pink. Andrew was really nervous that Roger would make him repaint the whole space the following week.

WINDOW TREATMENT Michelle's bargain drapes hung down to the floor. She explained, "Even if windows don't go to the floor, the drapes should. You can camouflage with lace, or sheer curtains or blinds so that it's not apparent where the window ends and the wall starts." The furniture was appropriate, but needed jazzing up. Another one of Michelle's bargain decisions was to spend $2 on brass-coloured thumb tacks that were applied in a pattern on the bedframe and night tables to brighten the dark walnut and give the pieces a new life.

ACCESSORIES Since the room was so large, it needed extra accessories. Michelle scoured flea markets, yard sales and second hand stores to come up with some bargains. For example, an old lamp was spray painted green. Then Michelle showed Suzanne how to make a matching lampshade by taking an inexpensive pleated shade and cutting off the pleated layer to leave a plain shade underneath. The pleated section was then used as a pattern to create a new shade made of prepasted white and green wallpaper, which was glued on the shade base and trimmed with green rick-rack. Michelle also found a round mirror that Genia fit inside an MDF square frame.

HOW TO MARBLING PAINT TECHNIQUE

2 colours of paint (one lighter and one darker — oil or latex)

varnish or urethane

2 small paint brushes or artist's brushes

1 plastic bag

1 feather

Paint one section of the item you're marbling with a base coat of paint (use either the lighter or darker paint colour).

Form the plastic bag into a ball and dab it lightly into the second paint colour, then gently dab on top of the base coat.

Drag the feather through the lighter colour and carefully draw marble veins.

Using a dry brush, soften the veins by gently dabbing them.

When the entire surface is marbled, paint a coat of varnish or urethane for a glossy look.

DAY 2

FIREPLACE All this was very well, but "French Country never seems complete to me without a fireplace," Michelle said. However, the only fireplace she could find within her budget was an ugly fake brick version for $100. Genia suggested hopefully that it might be easier to build a new fireplace, but Michelle liked the look of the brick and wanted to retain the character of the firebox. So Genia was called in to disguise what was there by using MDF to reface all but the faux brick features on the front. Michelle then painted the fireplace using a faux marble technique. (See how-to box on the previous page.) They also used a marbling technique on the mirror frame. Finally, Suzanne and Michelle used twigs and coloured cellophane to create a faux fire for their faux fireplace.

AFTER **A BRAND NEW CENTREPIECE**

THE RESULT What was Roger and Kim's reaction? They love their room and later called Michelle to say how restful it is for them. And a relieved Andrew was spared from repainting the walls the following week. As Michelle said, "Colour gives the biggest bang for the buck. As long as the colours are dancing to the right tune, you'll have your look."

AFTER NICE AND COSY, LIKE A COUNTRY INN

BUDGET

Bedding, Cushions, Pillows	$187.46	Throw Rug		$34.49
Fabric for Chair, Cupboards	$186.07	Lamps (second hand)		$15.00
Fabric and Tassels	$100.97	Tacks, Greenery		$10.35
Fireplace Mantel (second hand)	$100.00	Lights		$5.75
Drapes and Mirrors		Accessories		$4.60
(second hand)	$55.00	Tea Pot (second hand)		$3.00
Wallpaper	$52.50	Markers		$2.30
Fabric and Trim	$46.00	Carpenter's Expenses		$116.94
Accessories	$38.53			
		TOTAL (EXCLUDING PAINT)		**$1058.96**

THE CHALLENGE Two friends recently moved next door to each other, into two identical downtown townhouses. Decorating their new homes was fun until they reached the bedrooms, which were small and quite uninspiring. Penny Simmons said, "I haven't done a thing with the look of my bedroom or the furniture in it for 20 years. I feel like I've been carrying around the same furniture since I left home. I want someplace airy but cozy, where I can relax. And I don't want pink." Mari Lynn Knudsen said she also wanted a bright and airy room, that would be feminine, but not fussy and nothing too lacy.

PERSONAL RETREAT

THE GOAL Take two identical rooms belonging to two very different people and turn them into soothing personal spaces, reflecting each personality.

THE TEAM For Mari Lynn's room, Penny and her friend Pamela Roper, with designer Karen Adler and carpenter Graeme Kelly. For Penny's room, Mari Lynn and her friend Barbara Soutar, with designer Jane Hall and carpenter Bill Crossman.

BEDROOMS

THE SOLUTION TO MARI LYNN'S ROOM Mari Lynn had some fine artwork in her room and Karen decided to take her direction from one of the paintings. "A good tip is to look around and see what's in a person's home, then go from there. Building on things you love is really the way to decorate a room."

BEFORE **TOO COLD AND BARE**   AFTER **WARM, FEMININE AND FULL OF PERSONALITY**

DAY 1

FABRIC Mari Lynn's furniture is traditional and that helped to set the theme. A lot of fabric would be required to achieve the traditional, high-end look Karen envisioned. She decided to go with blue for the fabrics, selecting a marine blue with a *fleur de lis* pattern for the slipcover, a coordinating striped blue for curtains, and blue and white checks for the valance that Graeme would be building. Pamela was nominated to tackle all the sewing, beginning with the slipcover for Mari Lynn's tub chair.

WALLS Karen chose CIL Dulux latex flat paints in Nevada Sun, a soft, warm peach shade (20YY 61/231), for the walls, and Tusk (30YY 79/070), an off-white for the baseboards and windows. Renée loved the colours. "Very different from the fuchsia pink over at your place," she told Penny. "What's happening next door?" Penny was worried. "Think I'll go for a little walk," she said. "Could you hold this brush for just a minute?"

HEADBOARD Penny didn't need to worry about pink walls, since her room was being tastefully painted in cream. When she returned from her walk, Penny and Karen got to work on a headboard that Graeme had cut out of a piece of MDF. Karen had bought an art poster, Claude Monet's *Water Lilies at Giverny*, to use as an innovative and affordable decorative element. Karen and Penny spread adhesive on the back of the poster and then mounted it on the MDF board. They varnished the poster and Penny used gold paint to gild the picture frame. (See how-to box.) The bed, with its canopy and headboard, would be the focal point for the room.

HOW TO ART HEADBOARD

1

large art print	small half-round beading molding	finishing nails and counter sink
1 piece of ½-inch MDF cut to the size of the art print plus 3 inches on each side	Hodge Podge	wood filler
	paper glue	hammer
	gold paint	paint brushes and rags
molding — we used a 3-inch piece of carved molding but feel free to experiment	black acrylic paint	mitre saw
	raw umber	picture hooks
	glazing medium	

2

Glue the print to the MDF, making sure to carefully roll out any air bubbles. Let dry.

Paint the moldings with gold paint and let dry.

Once everything is dry, cut the 3-inch molding with the mitre saw to frame in the print. The wider edge of the molding should be flush with the edge of the piece of MDF.

3

Attach the molding to the MDF with finishing nails. If the corners do not match, fill with wood filler. Let dry, sand and touch up.

Fill all the nail holes with wood filler. Let dry, sand and touch up.

4

Make another frame within a frame using the half-round molding. Place this against the inside of the 3-inch molding to give added dimension. If this piece is very small use glue to attach instead of nails.

Mix a small amount of raw umber into a glazing medium and lightly brush over the entire picture to age and seal.

5

Rub the gold frame with a small amount of black acrylic to add to the aged effect — this is a simple rubbing technique where you apply the black paint and then rub most of it off, leaving the black in the cracks and crevices.

Attach to the wall with picture hooks.

6

DAY 2

VALANCE Day Two found Karen and Graeme looking concerned about the valance Graeme had been working on. The wood was a piece of scrap that Karen had found, but now she was afraid it was too thin. "It looks too wimpy," she said. "We need to make it more gutsy." Graeme assured her he could find extra wood scraps for free to double its sides. That calmed Karen's budget concerns.

FABRIC After the valance was bulked up, Karen attached quilt batting to the outside and then covered it with the blue and white checked fabric. Karen advises putting fabric on the inside of the valance as well as the outside so that the valance looks finished from the perspective of someone lying on the bed.

AFTER **THE VALANCE AND HEADBOARD ART REALLY MAKE A DIFFERENCE**

STAMPING Pamela was rescued at last from the sewing machine and recruited into stamping. Karen gave her a *fleur de lis* stencil, to coordinate with the slipcover fabric, that she would apply in white on the walls just under the ceiling. When Renée stopped to watch, they debated whether to add gold as a second colour around the stencil. Renée suggested that the white alone would match the baseboards and the window frame. "It's very subtle," she said and Pamela agreed.

PILLOW Karen showed Penny how to transfer another photocopied picture onto fabric. They used the fabric panel to make an elegant pillow for a total cost of about $10, including $1.50 for the photocopy. "A pillow like this would normally sell for $50," said Karen.

THE SOLUTION TO PENNY'S ROOM Jane had decided on a fantasy theme in blues and greens, with wonderfully textured laces, velvets, brocades and silky sari material. Since Penny's furniture was a hodge-podge of different styles and eras, Jane decided to pull everything together by painting it all in soft colours. She also took inspiration from a painting with a marvellous blue, and from Penny's work in the shoe business.

BEFORE **CLUTTERED**   AFTER **RICH AND INTERESTING**

DAY 1

FABRIC But first things first, and in this case it was getting started on the walls, painting them a soft blue-tinged green, CIL Dulux latex satin (70GG 32/067), with a golden cream latex satin (30YY 65/171) for the trim. Mari Lynn and Barbara took up their brushes and rollers. And Jane began painting a chair. "I got started painting floor cloths because I was intrigued to paint on canvas. I had this chair upholstered in canvas, primed the frame and the canvas and now I'm using acrylic paints. When I'm finished painting, I'll varnish." The chair was designed to become a special accent piece.

HOW TO ORNATE DRAPERY HEADBOARD

1

2

3

drill with countersinking bits

wood glue

screws

wall anchors

18 inches of 1 1/2-inch doweling

1 18-inch length of doweling

3 round wooden disks, at least 5 inches in diameter

3 carved wooden round pieces of detail molding to fit on top of the disks

3 pieces of 1/2-inch MDF cut into rectangular pieces measuring 3 1/2 inches x 1 1/2 inches

paint

sari fabric (or fabric of choice)

Paint all the wooden pieces. We used a gold paint on the carved detail molding and painted everything else deep teal.

Cut the dowel into three 6-inch pieces.

Place a wooden disk on top of the dowel, making sure that the dowel is in the centre of the circle.

Using the countersink bit, drill a hole so that it goes through the centre of the disk into the dowel.

Attach the disk to the dowel with a screw — make sure that the hole is countersunk to the point that the screw head will be flush to or lower than the top of the disk.

Place the dowel in the centre of the square of MDF. Turn it upside down and pre-drill a hole through the MDF and into the dowel.

4

Before attaching the MDF to the dowel, pre-drill holes 1/2 an inch from each side to attach the finial to the wall.

Screw the MDF to the dowel, making sure that the screw is either flush to or below the surface of the wood.

Glue the gold piece of molding to the centre of the wooden disk and let dry.

Repeat with the other 2 pieces.

Pick a spot on the wall that's over the centre of the bed. The middle finial will be affixed here, with the other 2 finials positioned slightly lower on either side corresponding with the sides of the bed. Attach the finials using screws and anchors through the pre-drilled holes in the MDF.

Drape your fabric over the finials in a tent-like fashion for an elegant effect.

DAY 2

PAINTING FURNITURE Day Two at Penny's house and Bill was making rope handles for a chest Jane would hand-paint. Mari Lynn and Barbara were learning how to give Penny's furniture an antique, tea-stained look using a darker cream paint, mixed with glaze. Jane would later use dark green paint for designs on the drawers.

FRENCH DRESSER In the backyard, Mari Lynn and Barbara had 24 dresser drawers to distress. Jane demonstrated how to use graphite paper to transfer a design right onto the wood for painting. The result, she assured them, would be a romantic French look. With another 23 drawers to complete, they weren't so sure.

FABRIC Jane had spent $90 on 18 yards of pale olive green sari material for the windows and for around the bed. Using finials Bill made, Jane draped the fabric around the bed like a canopy. (See how-to box, previous page.) Once this was in place, Jane produced her grand finale finishing touch — six very stylized drawings of shoes that she had photocopied and then framed in silver frames for a total cost of $150.

THE RESULT Some greenery and small accessories were added to complete Mari Lynn's room. "When you have a small budget, come up with a focal point and spend your money on it. And make it big," Karen said. "In this case, fabric changed the look of the room tremendously."

Next door, Penny was thrilled with her room, especially since it wasn't pink. And she loved the shoe prints. Jane said fabric and colour make all the difference. "Colour gives the biggest bang for the buck while fabric adds texture and visual interest."

Renée gave the final summations. For Mari Lynn's room: "What started with a white canvas, turned into a warm summer landscape." And at Penny's house: "Scene one was a bare stage; the finale was a rich theatrical production."

BUDGET
MARI LYNN'S ROOM

Fabric for Curtains, Tassels	$205.59	Bedskirt	$45.99
Frame, Plant Stand	$195.45	Pillow Shams	$43.10
Patterns for Chair, Ottoman	$150.50	Monet Poster	$38.81
Duvet	$103.49	MDF for Frame	$35.19
Curtain Rod, Brackets, Finial	$75.70	Fabric for Pillows, Thread	$22.97
Fabric for Valance	$50.84	Carpenter's Expenses	$143.82
		TOTAL (EXCLUDING PAINT)	**$1111.45**

BUDGET
PENNY'S ROOM

Fabric	$174.21	Chair Frame	$90.00
Sewing Supplies	$155.15	Chair Back	$52.43
Silver Frames, Prints	$150.67	Tassels	$22.99
Dresser	$140.00	Hat Boxes	$21.99
Frame	$124.09	Accessories	$12.05
		TOTAL (EXCLUDING PAINT)	**$943.58**

THE CHALLENGE Perry and Erin Zopf's bedroom is long and narrow, almost twice as long as it is wide, with heavy pine furniture. Because of the room's dimensions and the size of the furniture, there is little flexibility in rearranging or better utilizing the space. Erin said she had come to a complete standstill in trying to decorate the room to make it warm and inviting, not dull and awkward. "I need some magic," she explained. Perry said he was pretty agreeable to most changes except, "I'm not really into hot pink."

DRAMATIC DEEP COLOUR

THE GOAL To turn a bland, neutral and awkward bedroom into a comfortable and inviting retreat.

THE TEAM Erin's cousin Heather and her husband Alan McRobert, along with designer Evelyn Eshun and carpenter Genia Fromme.

BEDROOM

THE SOLUTION When Evelyn saw the Zopfs' pale yellow bedroom she decided that what was needed was colour, strong colour, to balance out the large furniture. "Since there wasn't the budget to buy new furniture, my strategy was to create atmosphere in the room. I wanted to make it cozy and relaxing," she said. Evelyn took the inspiration for the colour scheme from the couple's new bedding, which she purchased. The walls would be painted CIL Dulux Widow's Walk latex eggshell (50RR 14/045), a warm, deep purple.

BEFORE **OUTDATED FURNITURE WITH PALE WALLS**   AFTER **A PICK-ME-UP IN PURPLE**

DAY 1

CROWN MOLDING The team prepared for action. Heather and Alan removed the existing wallpaper border around the ceiling while Evelyn taped the walls. Genia was already busy cutting lengths of crown molding, which would add some architectural detail and give a sense of height to the room.

PAINTING FURNITURE With the painting well underway, Evelyn left Alan rolling and got Heather started on updating the pine furniture. This was going to be tricky. "The furniture is a bit of a challenge," Evelyn said. "We'll paint only parts of it, just to freshen it up." Heather looked doubtful. "It makes me nervous to paint wood," she explained. And what would Perry say? Heather wasn't too sure that he wanted his furniture altered. Nevertheless, she bravely began applying CIL Dulux Deep Onyx oil satin (00NN 05/000), a rich charcoal black, to the furniture frames. Since the furniture was clear-coated with oil, an oil paint had to be used.

DETAILS Back in the bedroom, Genia was cutting trim and fitting it around the doors.

BEFORE & AFTER FROM LIFELESS AND DRAB TO RELAXING

HOW TO FOLIAGE ART

1

choice of foliage (fern fronds, fall leaves, half-dried flowers, etc.)

iron and ironing board

2 clean tea towels or cloth napkins

wax paper

craft glue

2

art paper (will be used as a background so pick a colour that will complement your foliage)

frame

Before you start make sure that the foliage you are using is neither too dry nor too wet. Set your iron to a medium setting.

Place one of the tea towels on the ironing board.

3

Place a piece of wax paper on top of the tea towel with the waxed side up (this is the side that is more matte).

Place a couple of leaves on one side of the wax paper and fold the other side over so that it is covering the leaves.

Place the other tea towel over the wax paper and iron the entire surface for 30–45 seconds.

4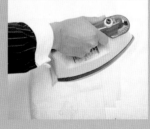

Remove your leaves. They should now be preserved with a coat of wax on each side.

Continue with the remaining leaves.

Cut the art paper to fit the frame.

Arrange the foliage in a pleasing design in the centre of the art paper and glue it using the craft glue.

5

Place the foliage art in the frame and hang.

DAY 2

PAINTING By early morning on Day Two Genia had finished installing the baseboard trim, so it was ready to be painted CIL Dulux Natural White latex satin (50YY 83/029). The ceiling molding and the door trim would also be painted white. Evelyn varnished some mirrors in a soft bronze for a glossy new look. Alan began to paint the trim and Heather finished a second coat on the furniture.

FOLIAGE ART Then Evelyn went outside to collect some leaves that would be waxed and framed for an inexpensive piece of artwork. (See how-to box, previous page.) Renée, checking in on the team's progress, found herself ironing leaves wrapped in waxed paper. "We used to do this in kindergarten," she said.

STENCILLING In the garage, Heather decided to solve the problem of tacky furniture, a damp day and a fast approaching deadline with a handy hair dryer. Back upstairs, Evelyn showed Alan how to add more interest to the walls by borrowing the diamond pattern from the bedding and stencilling diamonds on the wall, adding subtle texture with a high gloss varnish. (See how-to box, next page.)

FABRIC Evelyn hung panels of bright chartreuse fabric on swing rods attached to the wall on each side of the bed The windows got special treatment with more fabric panels, this time in a rich caramel colour, mounted on rods right below the crown molding to add more height and also some softness to the room.

FINISHING TOUCHES When the bed was finally in place, the framed leaf art, with its own halogen light fixture, was hung over the headboard. This added another focal point, said Evelyn, and a level of light that is so important when trying to create atmosphere. Some throw pillows on the bed and greenery in wall sconces completed the dramatic new look.

THE RESULT Erin and Perry were delighted with what Evelyn had achieved. "The key is colour," she said. "Colour can create such atmosphere — it's a great design tool. And deep colours are great in bedrooms for people who are uncertain about using strong colour elsewhere in the house."

BUDGET

Drapes	$174.20	Sconces	$57.78
Bedding	$137.00	Greenery	$50.61
Lamps	$100.00	Pillows	$37.93
Mirrors	$83.83	Tree	$28.49
Curtain Rods	$83.68	Carpenter's Expenses	$43.01
		TOTAL (EXCLUDING PAINT)	**$851.38**

HOW TO REVERSE STENCILLING TECHNIQUE

1

ruler, preferably metal

tape measure

level

utility knife

pencil

one sheet of mylar — quite thick so that it will hold its pattern

square

paint brush

paint tray

rollers and sleeves

low-tack painter's tape

paint

high gloss Varathane

2

3

4

5

Wash walls in preparation for painting.

Paint the walls with a base colour of your choice. For this technique it is better to use a darker colour as the Varathaned pattern will contrast better.

While the base coat is drying, make your stencil. Measure the width of the feature wall (the wall people's eyes will focus on as they come into the room) to determine how large the diamonds should be. The width of the diamond should divide evenly into the length of the wall. The diamonds should be between 8 inches and 12 inches wide.

Once you have decided on the width of the diamond, divide this number in half and write it down.

Find the exact centre of the mylar and make a dot to mark it.

Using the ruler and a level mark a spot on either side of the centre dot that is half the diamond width (the measure-ment you wrote down) away from the centre dot. Mark these spots with dots (make sure these marks are level with each other).

Repeat, marking dots above and below the centre dot. These are the 4 points of your diamond.

Using the square, connect the dots to make a diamond.

Cut the diamond shape out with a sharp utility knife and ruler. You now have your stencil.

On the wall find the level where you'd like to place your diamond border. Make a level line with a light pencil mark along the wall.

Starting at the corner of the wall, place the stencil so that the centre dot lines up with the pencil line. Tape the stencil to the wall with the low-tack tape.

Erase the pencil line.

Paint the area inside the stencil with high gloss Varathane. Try to use the Varathane sparingly so that it doesn't bleed, and always brush in the same direction.

Let the varathane dry a bit and remove the stencil. If there are bleed marks, don't worry, they can be touched up with the base coat paint once the pattern has dried.

Continue in the same manner along the wall until the border is complete.

THE CHALLENGE Carol and Chris Minos had a new home in a new subdivision and were happily expecting their first child. But the baby's room was bare except for a crib, dresser and rocking chair. It needed some great ideas and inspiration to make it more inviting.

CHILD-PERFECTING A

THE GOAL Create a soft, cozy, comfortable atmosphere for the new arrival.

THE TEAM The Minos' neighbours Shelley and Danny Sougaris with designer Karen Adler and carpenter Paul Trebilcock.

NURSERY

THE SOLUTION Since Carol and Chris didn't know whether a boy or a girl was on the way, Karen played it safe by finding wonderful, child-perfect fabric — a mouse-patterned print in baby yellow and pale blue. That established the room's colour scheme.

BEFORE **NO INSPIRATION HERE**   AFTER **A PRIMARY PALETTE AND FABRIC BRING THE ROOM TO LIFE**

DAY 1

WALLS The team began by painting over the pale lavender walls. Danny carefully painted the edges while Shelley exuberantly rolled along the top half of each wall with CIL Dulux Nursery Yellow (60YY 79/252), a latex eggshell. A tape around the middle of the walls indicated where the yellow would end and sky blue Sunday Sanala (70BG 72/086) would begin and continue to the floor.

BUNNY LIGHT Dramatic décor is for older people; small touches are a better scale to add charm to a baby's room, explained Karen. She started work on a plain, inexpensive lamp, enlisting Shelley to help turn it into a bunny light. They tied three plush bunny toys to the base with a decorative cord. Shelley then stenciled a random pattern on the shade using blue, yellow, and green paints that had been mixed with white paint to make them lighter. When the paint was dry, Shelley used a glue gun to attach powder blue pompom balls as a trim around the bottom of the shade. "It's so easy," said Karen. "And a lamp like this can cost up to $60 in a store." Her version cost $25.

WINDOW BENCH Paul and Danny installed a window bench that Paul had built, and Renée volunteered to sew a cover for the seat cushion using a waffle fabric in white and yellow checks. Paul's window seat gave the room a focal point and provided plenty of storage space, with shelves underneath to hold wooden toy boxes. Danny, following Karen's instructions, added a whimsical touch to the boxes, painting them in a variety of patterns. (See how-to box.)

SPECIAL TOUCHES Karen sewed a canopy for the baby's crib in sheer blue material. She then combined the blue fabric with the mouse print fabric to make curtains and a panel for the closet. Shelley sewed scraps of the mouse print into panels for small cushions. The room was starting to come together very nicely.

HOW TO MULTI—PATTERNED DRAWERS

an unfinished children's dresser (ours was a three drawer unit)

low-tack painter's tape in various widths

small rollers and sleeves

1-inch paint brushes

artist's brushes

faux finishing comb

primer

paint — we used

1 quart 60YY 79/252 Nursery Yellow latex eggshell

1 quart 70BG 72/086 Sunday Sanala latex eggshell

1 quart 30GY 72/196 Venetian Glass latex eggshell

DRESSER

Paint the dresser with a coat of primer.

Let dry and then give the unit, not the drawers, two coats of the colour of your choice.

DRAWERS

The triangle pattern

Paint the whole drawer with the base coat colour, using two coats if necessary. Let dry.

Once dry, start to tape off the pattern. Using 1-inch low-tack tape, tape from the upper left corner to the middle of the bottom edge. Then tape from the upper right corner to the middle of the bottom edge. Repeat this pattern from bottom corners to the middle of the upper edge. You should be left with a whole triangle in the middle flanked by 6 half diamonds.

Burnish the edges of your tape. (See page 103.)

Paint the 2 half diamonds along the top edge and the 2 half diamonds along the bottom edge a contrasting colour, making sure to stay within the taped areas.

Using a different contrasting colour, paint the 2 half diamonds and whole diamond that run across the middle of the drawer.

Let dry and paint with a second coat if necessary. Once completely dry, remove tape and replace drawer.

The plaid pattern

Paint the whole drawer with the base coat, using 2 coats if necessary. Let dry completely.

To make the plaid pattern, use the low-tack tape to create horizontal stripes of various widths, from very narrow to up to 1 inch wide.

Burnish the edges of the tape and paint each exposed stripe, alternating between the other 2 colours.

Remove the tape and let dry completely.

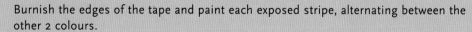

Once dry, repeat the process vertically, but this time include the base coat colour when you paint the different stripes. Remove the tape. Touch up any bleeding using the artist's brushes and let dry completely before replacing drawers in dresser.

DAY 2

CHANGE TABLE Danny and Paul built a versatile change table. It was secured to the wall through a wall joint, using a special hinge so it could accommodate the weight of the baby. For extra safety, the table was also secured to the wall with chains. The table was designed so that it could fold up when not in use, and it could be easily removed when it was no longer needed. The base of the table was covered in — what else? — the mouse print fabric and edged with blue pompom trim.

FINISHING TOUCHES The final touches were the rattle finials, small stuffed-toy rattles that were installed to hold the curtain rods on the wall. (See how-to box.)

HOW TO BABY RATTLE WINDOW SCONCES

4 colourful baby rattles (handles must be large enough to thread sheer material through)

4 3-inch dowels (1–2 inches thick)

2-inch nails

hammer

two 6-foot lengths sheer curtain material

two 6-foot lengths of 1-inch x 2-inch wooden rods cut to fit the length of each window

two 6-foot lengths of 1-inch x 2-inch wooden rods cut to fit the length of each window

Paint your dowel with colour of your choice.

Nail one dowel to each end of the wooden rods.

Nail each baby rattle just above the handle onto each dowel.

Thread your curtain material through the sconces and drape in a decorative fashion.

Nail the wooden rod just above each window.

BUDGET

Fabric for Curtains	$297.32	Toys, Stuffed Animals	$71.21
Crib Set	$129.35	Lightbulbs	$19.25
Hardware	$84.87	Carpenter's Expenses	$123.42
Fabric Trim	$80.40		
		TOTAL (EXCLUDING PAINT)	**$805.82**

THE RESULT Karen said it was fun to decorate the baby's room. Her primary expense was fabric, 32 yards of it, for curtains, canopy, and cushions. Her main challenge was designing the room so that it would continue to be functional for a growing child. "A baby is only a baby for a short period. You have to think ahead and add enough interest to the room. For instance, the two-toned walls will go from a newborn look to a juvenile look very easily." Carol and Chris agreed that the look was a big improvement on the previous bare room. It was charming and cozy, ready for their baby.

AFTER **THIS COLOURFUL NURSERY IS READY FOR BABY**

THE CHALLENGE At a certain point in every baby's life, it's time to move from the crib to a kid's bed, from rattles to teddy bears from soft pastels to bolder colours. Sam and Sophia Papadopoulos' one-year-old daughter Susanna was ready to take that big step. But she needed the proper setting and the bareness of a spare bedroom would not do. Her parents wanted her to have a special room, a place that would be fun, that would entice her to touch things. They also wanted the window seat in the room to become her private little nook and thinking spot. They emphasized that they didn't want wallpaper or too much pink.

A CHEERY TODDLER'S

THE GOAL To create a vibrant and welcoming room that would make anybody want to be a kid again.

THE TEAM Sam's sister and brother-in-law, Rita and Luis Leal, with designer Tammy Schnurr and carpenter Genia Fromme.

BEDROOM

THE SOLUTION Lots of colour — that was Tammy's first thought when faced with this decorating challenge. So the team began with a colour wash on all the walls, using CIL Dulux Lemon Zest latex flat (46YY 74/602), a bright yellow. They mixed four parts paint, one part glaze and one part water. They ragged this mixture on all the walls, in a circular motion to avoid a flat appearance. When the colour wash had dried, the team taped off one wall into four squares. Each square was painted a different colour using CIL Dulux semi-gloss Siesta Pink (53RR 27/417); Azure Blue (39BB 18/351); Niagara Mist turquoise green (85GG 44/328); and Poppy Glow gold orange (78 YR 39/593).

BEFORE **THE WINDOWS WERE LOST**   AFTER **COLOURFUL VALANCES PROVIDE FOCUS**

DAY 1

VALANCES While walls were being painted, Genia made valances for the four tall windows in the room, with the bottom of each valance cut out in a wave effect. The valances were then primed and each one painted a colour to match the four squares on the wall.

CHAIR With the painting well underway, Louis got to work sanding an antique chair that had been in the Papadopolous' garage. Later, Rita stained it to bring out the cherry wood.

RUG Meanwhile, Tammy got down to basics with a cotton rug she had bought for $10 at a garage sale. The rug was checked in squares, but to emphasize the shape and coordinate with the room, she taped off some of the squares to paint them the same colours that had been used for the squares on the walls. "A cotton rug absorbs the paint," Tammy explained to Louis when he offered to help. "I'm using latex paint, but you could also use acrylic or fabric paint." She left him to complete the job while she began sewing curtains using a bright semi-sheer fuchsia fabric.

HOW TO COLOUR BLOCK SHELVES

1

12 pieces of ½-inch MDF measuring 12 inches x 12 inches	duct tape	metal L-brackets
	wood glue and nails	painter's tape
	wood filler	level
paint	clamps	square
		table saw

2

With the table saw, mitre at 45 degrees two opposite sides of each of the pieces of MDF so that the mitres lean in toward each other.

To make the boxes, line up 4 of the mitred pieces, mitred side down. The mitred edges should be butted up against each other.

Take the duct tape and secure the pieces together.

3

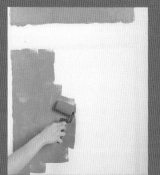

Turn over and place glue on the mitre cuts. Fold over into a box and tape the remaining joint. Place clamps on each side to hold in place. Nail the box together along each joint. Let dry.

Once dry, remove the clamps, sand off any excess glue and fill any holes with wood filler.

Sand, wipe clean and paint inside and out.

Decide where you would like to hang the boxes on the wall.

4

Using the level and square, draw squares on the wall measuring 24 inches x 24 inches. Tape them off using the painter's tape around the outside edge. Paint the interior with contrasting colours (see pictures).

Repeat paint coats. Remove tape after paint is dry. Place the shelving in the centre of the colour blocks and secure to the wall from the inside using metal L-brackets.

DAY 2

COLOUR Day Two started awash with colour as the team created their own special rainbow: two small pink wooden chairs here, a blue table there. Renée painted the stem of a lamp pink at the top and green in the middle, with a blue bottom and orange base. Its white pleated shade was then given the full floral treatment with pink and blue silk flowers randomly hot glued all over the surface. "The flowers cost 69 cents each and the lamp itself was under $20," said Tammy. Renée was impressed. "So for very little money, you were able to create some whimsy for this room," she said.

BOX SHELVES Genia was in the garage building box shelves. She showed Louis how to tape the shelves tightly together before gluing and nailing them. (See how-to box, page 85.) Then it was time for the paint team to prime and paint them using CIL Dulux White Mountain latex semi-gloss (50BB 83/020). When the shelves were dry, Genia hung each unit directly in the centre of one of the colour blocks on the walls. The shelves were filled with Susanna's teddy bears and other stuffed toys.

FABRIC A change table, bedside table and bookshelf, all roadside throwaway finds, were painted in semi-gloss white with some flowers and zoo animals painted on as decoration. Not finished yet, Tammy and Rita sewed about 20 pillows, in a variety of solid and plaid fabrics, for the window seat, the bed and to reupholster the antique chair. The same fabrics were used as matts for some picture frames Tammy had found and painted semi-gloss white. Tammy cut thick cardboard to fit the frames, cut the fabric a little larger than the frame size and sprayed adhesive to glue the fabric to the cardboard, folding the edges and then gluing the photo to the centre of the mat. "This is an easy and inexpensive way to coordinate a room," Tammy explained.

FINAL TOUCHES Finally, with the fuchsia curtains hung, the pillows piled on a turquoise bedspread on the bed, a combination of fuchsia, turquoise and orange pillows comfortably fitting in the window seat, and a small child's vanity that Tammy had bought for $125 set into place, the room was complete.

THE RESULT Since Susanna was only one year old she didn't say much, but Sophia was so pleased she got teary — although in a room so bright and cheery it's hard to do anything but smile.

BUDGET

Vanity	$125.00	Crib Bumper, Sheets	$36.00
Children's Chairs	$103.27	Ribbon	$23.53
Chair, Mirror (second hand)	$97.30	Curtain Rod	$15.94
Bed	$84.00	Sewing Supplies	$14.47
Accessories	$57.52	Frames	$12.62
Fabric	$49.65	Trim	$12.33
Lamp	$46.93	Carpenter's Expenses	$210.78
		TOTAL (EXCLUDING PAINT)	**$889.34**

THE CHALLENGE Once upon a time, Rita and Luis Leal's five-year-old daughter Nicolette was living in a bland room. It wasn't a bad room, but it was boring with a big queen-size bed, triple dresser, armoire and matching night tables. Basically, it just wasn't much fun for a little girl. Rita and Louis wanted to do something special for Nicolette. "Special, but not all pink," said Rita. But where would they begin?

A CINDERELLA

THE GOAL To wave a magic wand or other instruments of influence (paint brushes, for example) and turn this dull bedroom space into a fairy tale, totally-not-pink place complete with its very own multi-coloured rainbow.

THE TEAM Rita's brother, Sam, and his wife Sophia Papadopoulos, with designer Jan Kerr and carpenter Graeme Kelly.

BEDROOM

THE SOLUTION When Jan first saw the room she was pleased that it was in a new house, which meant that the team wouldn't have to deal with unusual floor designs or stripping wallpaper. But she was faced with a lot of large furniture that left little extra space for imaginative treatments. Her inspiration was a Cinderella print given by Sam and Sophia to Nicolette for her first birthday, and a new mauve and white comforter for the bed.

BEFORE **LIKE A HOTEL SUITE**   AFTER **A FAIRYTALE BEDROOM**

DAY 1

WALLS The team began with the walls, dividing them horizontally in half, and then painting the top half CIL Dulux Alarm Clock latex eggshell mauve and the bottom half Classic White latex eggshell. "This is such a fabulous colour," said Renée, as she brushed cool purple across the walls. "I'm having such a good time. When I was a little kid I never had a designer bedroom. I don't know about you." "Beige," said Sophia.

PLAYHOUSE Meanwhile, since every little princess needs her own castle, Graeme and Sam were preparing to build a castle playhouse in one corner of the room using a sketch Jan had drawn. First they cut out the shape of the castle from MDF board, saving the scraps as small blocks. These were attached to the castle walls to add dimension and simulate the look of stone. Now, the castle needed a grand entrance. "We'll make a 30-inch door," said Graeme. "That's a good height for a five-year-old." Graeme left Sam to cut out the doorway while he started attaching a chair rail around the walls to separate the white from the purple portions.

WINDOW TREATMENT Sophia was getting her own lessons in cutting from Jan, who wanted to use fanciful finials for the window curtains. "We'll swag the fabric behind them," Jan explained. She showed Sophia how to cut patterns from MDF for a glass slipper and a magic wand with a star. They would prime and paint these and attach them to the wall as brackets.

HOW TO **PLAID-PATTERNED WALLS**

1

base colour paint

paint for the plaid colour(s) of choice — complementary to the base colour. Please note: You may use one colour for your horizontal and vertical stripes, or add more depth by choosing two colours that are complementary to each other.

stucco roller sleeves (the ones that are made from a series of foam discs are best)

duct tape

2

Paint the walls with the base coat and let dry.

Decide how thick you want your plaid lines to be and prepare the roller.

Moving about an inch to an inch-and-a-half from the edge of the roller sleeve, wrap the duct tape as tightly as you can around the sleeve. Try to bind the foam as much as possible!

3

Continue this process along the length of the roller sleeve. Because this is a country look, don't try to make the raised sections identical, vary their width. You should have approximately 5 raised sections.

4

Carefully dip your roller in the paint tray, allowing the paint to coat ONLY those sections that are raised.

Starting with the vertical, roll the pattern onto the wall. Let dry.

Once the vertical stripes are dry, apply the horizontal stripes starting from the upper edge of the design and moving down.

5

DAY 2

PAINTING Day Two found everyone caught up in the mood of this enchanted kingdom (whoops, princess-dom). Jan and Sophia painted the finials white, making them funky with lots of purple dots, stars and squiggles. The next step was to paint a rainbow on the wall behind the castle, beginning with a wide arc of green, adding another arc of blue and above the two, an arc of cream. The castle itself was painted white with a purple roof.

AFTER **A MAGICAL PLACE TO REST**   AFTER **WHEN YOU'RE FINISHED ROAMING THE CASTLE**

PLAID WALLS While Jan stencilled white stars in galaxies across the purple areas of the walls, Sam and Sophia gave the white sections the plaid treatment. They began by tightly taping portions of two stucco rollers, leaving about five raised sections on each roller and then, dipping the rollers in the purple paint, they painted purple lines in a pattern that was not meant to be perfectly precise, across and up and down the walls. (See how-to box, previous page.)

FINISHING TOUCHES Jan had bought coordinating bed sheets in mauve and white with mauve polka dots. She cut them in half and folded them to use as curtains. Then she mounted cup hooks in the ceiling over the bed and attached layers of lace to create a canopy effect. Finally, using a fabric tip on a craft bottle and white latex paint, Jan wrote "Star light, star bright" and "Somewhere over the rainbow," around the walls, adding a few more constellations and similar objects to the astral scene. The Cinderella print was hung over the bed and a pair of glass slippers left at the entrance to the castle.

THE RESULT The total cost of the enchanted castle was only $40. The fabric was a bargain at $8 a yard. So, the team finished their work well satisfied and quite within budget in this lovely princess room. Nicolette loved her rainbow and they all lived happily ever after.

AFTER EVERYTHING A PRINCESS WOULD WANT

BUDGET

Fabric for Curtains	$315.65	Hardware	$29.32
Pillow, Accessories	$213.58	Cinderella Book	$8.55
Bedding	$73.56	Carpenter's Expenses	$124.68
Craft Stencil and Paints	$56.27		
		TOTAL (EXCLUDING PAINT)	**$821.61**

THE CHALLENGE Voula Kapralos is a university student living with her parents. Her room is an almost self-contained unit with a small kitchenette, on the upper floor of the house. That's the good news. The bad news is that the room had three definite drawbacks — it was large but L-shaped, one of the walls opened onto the two-storey landing area, and it was cluttered with the family cast-off furniture, heavy old pieces and worn hand-me-downs that were totally inappropriate for a young woman.

A STYLISH STUDENT

THE GOAL Create a stylish space, fresh and new, where Voula could happily spend time relaxing, studying, or entertaining her friends.

THE TEAM Voula's brother and sister-in-law, Jenny and John Kapralos, with designer Adriana Urtasun and carpenter Jason Kuczeryk.

BEDROOM

THE SOLUTION Adriana visualized contemporary and colourful. Colour was no problem with the paint palette she selected including CIL Dulux Jasmine Yellow latex flat (50YY 83/200-7) for the walls and latex satin Lichen Green (70YY 55/299-8), Pecan Tree brown (40YY 53/218) and hot Red Letter Day (10YR 15/500) to accent and accessorize. A contemporary look was a bit more more difficult since there was not enough money to buy new furniture and most of the furniture couldn't be reused. So Adriana chose fresh, crisp blue, yellow, green and grey fabrics, planning to slipcover whatever she could and store the rest.

BEFORE **FROM MISMATCHED HAND-ME-DOWNS**   AFTER **TO COORDINATED AND MODERN**

DAY 1

WALLS Adriana dealt with the size and shape of the room by creating different zones — a work zone with a desk, a private zone for the bed and an entertainment zone with a couch and coffee table. Carpenter Jason was assigned to build a new bed for Voula, with drawers underneath for extra storage space. Adriana found a large armoire that had been discarded. She immediately rescued it, proving once again that one man's trash is truly another man's (or in this case, woman's) treasure.

OPPORTUNITIES So while Jenny painted walls and Jason set to work building the bed, John sanded the armoire, preparing to paint it lichen green and pecan brown. Host Renée was assigned to sew bed linens and slipcovers. Problems became opportunities. When Jason's headboard was looking too thin, Adriana suggested a plywood trim on the top and sides to give a clean line.

MESSAGE BOARD Adriana decided to turn the opening overlooking the front hall into a large bulletin board. She and Jenny cut styrofoam boards to fit the space and then glued on material in a soft green shade. Once installed, this novel bulletin board would also act as a sound insulator.

AFTER CREATIVE TOUCHES ADD TO ANY SPACE

HOW TO PAINTED MIRRORS

1

4 square mirror tiles

painter's tape or masking tape

ruler

square

wax pencil

utility knife

foam brush

wet fine grit sandpaper

oil based paint in the colour of your choice

2

Clean the glass.

Measure 3 inches in from each edge and mark at various points with the wax pencil.

Using these marks as a guide, tape off a square inside the lines.

Make sure the mirror corners are at 90 degree angles with the square.

3

Burnish the tape and then use the utility knife to clean up any edges or corners.

Using the wet fine grit sandpaper lightly sand the exposed glass.

Wipe clean and paint with the oil paint and foam brush. Try to keep your brush strokes going in the same direction for a cleaner finish.

4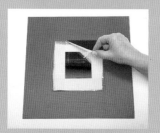

Let dry.

Remove the tape after first scoring between the tape and the paint with a utility knife.

Clean, hang and enjoy!

DAY 2

ACCESSORIES Day Two and it was time to spruce up the place with imaginative accessories. Adriana took a package of 12-inch by 12-inch mirrors, taped off a centre square and then painted the rest of each mirror bright red. When the tape was removed, she had funky faux framed mirrors. (See how-to box, previous page.)

FINISHING TOUCHES John fastened the bedframe to the wall while Jenny and Adriana made two upholstered cubes, each cube consisting of four pieces of heavy duty four-inch foam that was glued together. They covered the foam with green slipcovers to make coffee tables that can double as ottomans when Voula has guests (see how-to box.) Two orange swivel bar chairs, a bargain store find at $5 each, were placed around a small round white table and the room was ready for viewing.

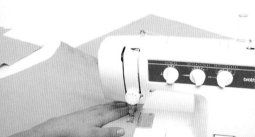  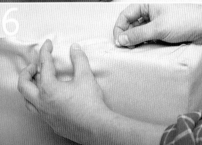

HOW TO CUBED COFFEE TABLE

4 pieces of upholstery foam , approximately 4 inches x 20 inches x 20 inches

spray adhesive

2 1/2 yards of fabric

Stack foam pieces together to create a cube. Attach the pieces with spray adhesive.

To make the cover, you'll need to cut 6 fabric panels. For the side panels, cut 4 pieces of fabric to 17 1/2 inches x 21 1/2 inches. For the top and bottom, cut 2 pieces of fabric to 21 1/2 inches x 21 1/2 inches.

Notch corners by measuring a half-inch point on both sides of each corner. Mark the two spots you measure. Cut inward from each point until the cuts meet to make a 1/2-inch notch.

Sew each of the side panels to the next, making a row.

Sew the far left edge of the first panel to the far right edge of the last panel, right fabric sides together. This will make a tube.

Sew the top panel to the top edge of all the sides (right sides together). Make certain that the needle of the sewing machine is resting at the point of the notch in each panel corner.

Sew one edge of the bottom panel to one bottom edge of one side, right sides together, leaving the other three sides open.

Turn tube-shaped cover right side out. Insert the cube form. Smooth out any twisted seams. Slip-stitch the three remaining edges of the bottom piece to the bottom edges of the open three sides.

THE RESULT Voula was thrilled with the new look. Adriana said it was a challenge because the L-shaped layout made the space almost like two rooms. She pulled them together by using a consistent, neutral colour palette and throwing in punches of colour with the red faux-framed mirrors and bright orange chairs. Adriana's advice is that when there's only a small budget, focusing on a few large pieces, in this case the bed and armoire, makes the biggest impact.

BUDGET

Fabric for Slipcovers	$365.83	Accessories, Hardware	$17.85
Chairs	$302.13	Chairs (second hand)	$10.00
Lamps	$145.11	Flowers	$6.88
Fabric for Bedding	$52.10	Carpenter's Expenses	$186.63
Fabric for Footstools	$37.20		
		TOTAL (EXCLUDING PAINT)	**$1123.73**

THE CHALLENGE Janet Smith, her husband and their two small children had lived in their home for more than two years but had done nothing, not even added matching towels, to the ensuite beige bathroom off the master bedroom. Janet didn't want to see bright colours or reds, and she preferred earthy tones to pastels. She was hoping for something a little fancier than what was already there but it had to be functional because the children use this bathroom, too.

SPA ASPIRATIONS

THE GOAL To create a spa-like retreat that would still be family friendly.

THE TEAM Next-door neighbours Lisa and Martin Kaefer, with designer Evelyn Eshun and carpenter Jeremy Plant.

BATHROOM

THE SOLUTION The good news was that the room was a neutral colour with white fixtures and no architectural details to deal with. That was also the bad news. Evelyn knew she would have to create architectural interest to add some charm. Her concept was a spa-like retreat.

BEFORE & AFTER **HORIZONTAL STRIPES ADD HEIGHT**   BEFORE & AFTER **ARCHITECTURAL CHARM**

DAY 1

CEILING The team began by taping and then painting the ceiling CIL Dulux latex eggshell Hope Blue (50BB 62/038). "A lot of people paint their ceilings white but when you use a colour like this blue, which we're used to seeing outside, it actually does raise the height of the ceiling," explained Evelyn. "It has a shimmer to it," Lisa said. "Yes, it's a soft blue," Evelyn agreed.

CABINETRY To cut down on the crowd in the room, Jeremy and Martin went outside to start building a bulkhead, a simple box frame that they would attach to the wall and ceiling over the vanity. Lisa wasn't far behind, taking the wall cabinet with her to paint it Widow's Walk, a deep taupe latex eggshell (50RR 14/045).

WALLS That left Evelyn alone to apply Castle Rock soft taupe latex eggshell (10YY 41/083) as a base coat for the horizontal, silver metallic stripes that would soon follow. Evelyn chose stripes because they would reflect the light and also alter the sense of space. She explained that the room would appear larger because of the scale of the stripes relative to the height of the walls. (See how-to box, next page.)

SPECIAL TOUCHES Once Lisa had finished the cabinet, she and Evelyn worked on decorating a frame that Martin had made out of MDF. This frame would become a hanging faux fireplace. (See how-to box, page 105.)

HOW TO **HORIZONTAL STRIPING**

1

paint for the base coat:
satin latex paint (CIL –
Castle Rock 10YY 41/083)

paint for the stripes: metallic
silver paint

low-tack painter's tape

paint tray

roller and roller cover

paintbrush

level

measuring tape

2

Paint the wall surface with the base colour.

Determine the width and direction of the stripes, keeping them in proportion to the room. Narrow stripes in a large room get lost, whereas a small room with large stripes looks out of proportion. Use a tape measure to mark off the stripes. Use a level to draw in a light pencil line from side to side.

3

Tape the areas not to be painted using a low-tack painter's tape that will peel off easily when the job is done. Burnish the edges of the tape by applying pressure along the tape edge (a thumb nail works well). Don't forget to tape off the ceiling, baseboard and any other trim that will come in contact with paint.

For this look, paint the stripes in long horizontal strokes to create the look of a master painter. The brushmarks will be soft and subtle. It will take a little longer than a roller but the look is worth it. Remove the tape as you paint the stripes to help prevent the paint from creeping under the tape.

4

If there is paint that has crept under the tape, use an artist's brush to touch up the lines.

COLOUR ADVICE

Generally, a large area covered with a stripe design calls for a subtle difference between the stripes. Use two colours from the same colour family, one about two or three shades from the other. A very elegant stripe can be created if you use a flat base coat then paint the stripes in the same colour using a semi-gloss sheen. Bold differences in stripes should be confined to smaller areas above or below trims and moldings.

DAY 2

MOLDING On Day Two Renée was roped in to help paint the molding Casbah, a dark brown latex eggshell (50YR 14/045). Evelyn said that adding a molding detail in a dark, contrasting colour adds depth and elegance. Meanwhile, Evelyn continued working on her elegant silver stripes.

CHANDELIER Martin escaped outside, avoiding the bathroom crowd, to cut a chandelier base from MDF in a flat doughnut shape.

AFTER DECORATIVE PANEL   AFTER A COSY PLACE FOR A CALM BATH

DECORATIVE PANEL The decorative panel was ready for painting so Evelyn showed Lisa how to take the Widow's Walk colour mixed with five parts glaze to one part paint, and rub the glaze on with a rag. When it dried, she mixed the silver paint that was being used for the striping in the same five-to-one proportion with the glaze and repeated the procedure to accent the decoration. The edging would be painted the same dark brown as the molding. Jeremy cut some leftover fluted molding to affix to the sides of the mirror, painting each piece dark brown, even the backs, since everything would be reflected in the mirror. They were then attached with silicone, which acts like glue on a mirror and dries clear. The bulkhead and the moldings gave the vanity mirror the illusion of a built-in unit.

FINISHING TOUCHES Martin's chandelier was painted in the bathroom colours and attached with aircraft cable to the ceiling. It could hold candles or tea lights to create a luxurious spa mood. The faux fireplace, complete with shelf and candles, was hung on the wall and yards of white and taupe curtains draped at the window and the shower stall.

BUDGET

Candle Holder, Hooks	$178.09	Chandelier (second hand)	$15.00
Fabric	$146.05	Candles	$9.18
Light Fixture	$143.70	Drawer Pulls	$8.74
Accessories	$88.12	Carpenter's Expenses	$313.12
Curtain Rods	$23.14		
		TOTAL (EXCLUDING PAINT)	**$956.98**

THE RESULT Evelyn said her biggest challenge was taking a relatively small bathroom and making it feel larger and more luxurious. "My best bargains were the Retro Art panel, the chandelier for $15 and definitely the fabric for window and shower curtains. And yes, we came within budget, even with all the candles we bought." Janet's reaction: "I just have to have a bath tonight!"

HOW TO **RETRO ART PANEL DETAIL**

1

Retro Art panel #4009 (2 feet x 4 feet), with glue provided

³/4-inch MDF cut to 2 ¹/2 feet x 6 feet

router and bits

carpenter's glue

paint for base coat

paint for top glaze

latex metallic silver paint

glaze

rags and brushes

picture hanging materials

2

Cut MDF to 3 inches larger than panel.

Using a router, shape and round the edges.

Cut out 4-inch deep shelf from remaining MDF.

Glue and screw shelf to main panel.

3

Glue Retro Art to panel with glue provided and let dry.

Paint with base coat colour. Let dry.

Glaze panel with five parts glaze to one part of second paint colour. Rub it on with a rag.

When dry, mix silver paint with glaze in the same proportion and repeat the procedure.

Once it's completely dry, hang picture.

4

5

THE CHALLENGE Sylvia and Keith Juriansz had a very large bathroom that was painted white with grey fixtures. Keith said he really didn't mind because he hardly ever got a chance to use it since his wife was in there all the time. But Sylvia disagreed, saying the bathroom was too dull and cold-looking. "I just want to shower and get out as fast as I can, it's not a relaxing atmosphere. As it stands now, the bathroom is ultra-modern and needs to be toned down a bit...more traditional but with a bit of pizzazz," she suggested hopefully.

COZYING UP A LARGE

THE GOAL Make the room warmer and more inviting, a place where Sylvia can relax in the spa tub and where Keith will want to spend some time.

THE TEAM Sylvia's older brother, Bob, and sister-in-law, Barbara, along with designer David MacPhee and carpenter Graeme Kelly.

BATHROOM

THE SOLUTION Everything that was movable was removed from the bathroom, including a large mirror over the sinks that accentuated the size of the room. David chose a warm French Yellow to paint the walls, deciding that it would go well with the fixtures, and White Mountain latex semi-gloss (50BB 83/020) for the trim. Then everybody got to work painting the room. But David wasn't content with simply introducing colour to the walls. That was only the beginning.

BEFORE **ZERO PERSONALITY**   AFTER **ARCHITECTURAL DETAIL BRINGS THE ROOM TO LIFE**

DAY 1

ARCHITECTURAL DETAILS David asked Graeme to add architectural details: crown molding bordering the ceiling and wainscoting closer to the floor. Then more molding was used to provide detail in small panels around the toilet and bidet area. These accents helped make the room less austere. The molding below the ceiling was painted white while the rest was painted yellow, blending in with the walls.

WHOOPS No project is without its incidents, of course, as Graeme discovered when he tried to remove the toilet paper holder from the wall. Not realizing his own strength, he pulled the holder and accidentally punched a hole in the wall. "We can just hang a picture to hide the hole," he offered helpfully. But David, clearly not amused, suggested that Graeme repair the damage right away since time was running out on Day One.

PAINTING TECHNIQUE Before they were ready to quit for the day, however, David and Barbara decided to tackle the challenge of adding a linen look to the wall area above the molding using Pineapple (45YY 68/380) latex semi-gloss over the freshly painted darker yellow base. David demonstrated the technique to Barbara who was eager to learn as many decorating tricks as possible. "It says we have an hour of open time before the glazing dries," David said. "But I don't believe it." So speed, as well as skill, was required as the two of them got busy dragging a brush with the paler yellow paint vertically and horizontally across the wall area. (See how-to box.)

HOW TO LINEN PAINT TECHNIQUE

1

dragging brush, such as a wallpaper brush

surfacing compound

lint-free cloth

2 shades of the same colour of latex paint, eggshell or semi-gloss (the shades should be 2 or 3 steps away from each other on the paint chip)

latex glazing liquid

2

Patch any holes and cracks in the wall with a putty knife and surfacing compound. Let dry, then sand smooth. Tape off all moldings, door and window casings. Protect floor with drop cloths.

Roll the walls with the darker colour. Let dry for at least 2 hours.

3

Mix 1 part of the lighter paint colour with 4 parts latex glazing medium in a large bucket. Try to mix enough for the whole wall so that the colour will be consistent.

Pour some of the mixture into a paint tray and roll it onto the wall in straight, 3-foot vertical strips from ceiling to floor. Starting at the top, slowly and firmly pull the dragging brush straight down the wall in one complete motion.

4

After each drag, wipe the brush with a clean, lint-free cloth to remove excess glaze. Continue with the 3-foot area, remembering to leave a wet edge.

After the stripes have been vertically dragged, drag the same brush horizontally across the area, keeping the brush level. This should leave a coarse, linen-like pattern. Continue the horizontal dragging until section is done.

5

Continue across the wall, overlapping the paint/glaze mixture into the wet edge. As you continue the horizontal lines, stagger the ends, leaving no definite end marks.

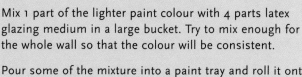

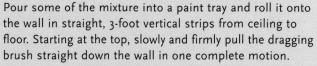

DAY 2

CABINET Day Two, and Graeme was building an open cabinet that would be painted the same sunny French yellow to hang over the sinks. It was Barb's turn to take charge as she hemmed yards of floral material, a white background with greens, reds and a yellow that matched the walls, for a window treatment and a complementary shower curtain.

LIGHTING New light fixtures were installed over the sink counter to warm the lighting in the room. Then two smaller mirrors were hung, replacing the larger one.

SOAP While this was going on, Bob was in the kitchen cooking up some soap. He started with a soap kit then added some soap shavings and colour. He put this mixture into the microwave oven for 45 seconds until it melted. Then he poured the liquid over lemon peels in one mold and poppy seeds in another. "It takes about 10 minutes to solidify," he said.

SILVER LEAF When Barbara finished her sewing, David put her to work applying silver leaf to an urn. First she brushed on some adhesive, then David showed her how to use the silver leaf. "It's very finicky work," he said. "The leaf is very thin and you have to try and control it. Brush it in, the creases and folds just add to the antique look we're trying to create."

TOWEL RACK The final project was a standing towel rack made out of a newel post with round towel rings attached. (See how-to box.) "We made the towel rack to use up space and also to place the towels closer to the tub," David said. New towels and some small carpets matching the yellow colour scheme were arranged around the room. A plant was set in the silvered urn, and Bob's soaps adorned the sink counter. Elegant.

FINISHING TOUCHES David said, "The first thing you have to do when decorating a room is establish a theme or direction and then buy the most expensive item first (in this case it was the window and shower curtain fabric at $250). Once I know the cost of this, I continue to finish the room with architectural details and accessories, depending on what money I have remaining." The two mirrors were $35 and the light fixtures were $25.

THE RESULT When Sylvia saw her new bathroom she said it was better than she could ever have imagined. Then she spied the bathtub with water already drawn for a bath. "This is wonderful," she told David. "You're never leaving this house."

BUDGET

Fabric	$230.01	Towel Rings, Hooks	$69.39
Hardware	$122.39	Rods	$41.09
Accessories	$109.35	Towels	$35.00
Stencils, Stencilling Paint	$91.00	Cedar Posts	$26.68
Light fixtures	$89.88	Craft Supplies	$17.20
Mirrors	$76.25	Carpenter's Expenses	$166.47
		TOTAL (EXCLUDING PAINT)	**$967.71**

HOW TO STANDING TOWEL RACK

a wooden banister or newel post

3 round towel rings

16-inch x 16-inch MDF square base

4 screws

Using saw, cut bottom 3 inches off of newel post.

Attach banister/post to MDF square base with screws.

Paint as desired.

Mount towel rings onto sides of banister/post.

THE CHALLENGE What's to be done with an open hallway at the top of the stairs that's too large to waste but awkward to furnish? That was the problem that stumped Lisa and Martin Kaefer. They were hoping for a solution that would include a fairly formal look and neutral tones. They knew their space had potential. Could *The Decorating Challenge* uncover its true worth?

A LANDING READING

THE GOAL To turn the Kaefers' landing into a family-friendly, useful place.

THE TEAM Next-door neighbour Janet Smith with her friend Sarah Heuls standing in for Janet's husband who was babysitting the Smiths' children, with designer David MacPhee and carpenter Graeme Kelly.

LIBRARY

THE SOLUTION David was intrigued by the space because it was so large and also quite bright, with windows along the outside wall. And all that nice, natural light gave David his novel idea to create a reading/library area on the landing.

BEFORE IN NEED OF A DESIGNER'S TOUCH

AFTER A LIBRARY FOR THE WHOLE FAMILY

DAY 1

WALLS The first challenge was to keep the space separate but to blend it in since it was open to the rest of the house. That could be achieved by painting metallic stripes on the wall using colours from the rest of the house. So Janet and Sarah began by measuring the wall for the stripes while David assigned Graeme to create false bookshelves on the outside of the linen closet doors by gluing on pieces of MDF.

BOOKCASES A lot of stripes means a lot of taping on the walls. Renée offered to help, despite David's teasing about her taping skills. So Janet and Renée completed the taping while Graeme went outside to assemble the first of two actual bookcases. Then Janet started painting the walls CIL Dulux latex eggshell Camelcoat (20YY 43/200), a soft peachy beige.

SPECIAL TOUCHES David had bought several boxes of used hardcover books for a special effect he was planning. Stacking some on the table, he told Sarah he needed her to help trim off the spines He showed her how to cut them very slowly with a craft knife, keeping the spines intact. "There are mountains of books outside. I'll go get some more," he said. All those books and absolutely no time for reading.

ARCHITECTURAL DETAILS Meanwhile, Graeme installed two pillars on the landing. "This is a neoclassic house with a lot of pillars in it already. Putting two on the landing will provide some architectural detail for the space," David explained. The pillars and the bookshelves were painted White Mountain latex eggshell (50BB 83/020).

HOW TO **FAUX BOOKSHELF ON CLOSET DOORS**

plenty of old hardcover books from garage sale or second hand store

five 8-foot lengths of 1-inch x 1-inch trim to create faux shelves

2 doors (new closet doors can be bought or existing closet doors can be used as long as they're not sliding doors)

two 8-foot lengths of 4-inch flat molding or baseboard for top and bottom of each door

six 8-foot lengths of $\frac{3}{4}$-inch trim to be nailed around frame of each door

mitre saw

router and bits (or jig saw)

hammer

2-inch finishing nails

one gallon of primer

one gallon of light or white interior flat latex paint to cover the doors, trim and molding

paint roller and paint tray

4 door handles — appropriate size and colour for your shelves

4 hinges (only if hanging new doors)

utility knife

glue gun and glue sticks

tea bag (for stain)

small paint brush

1

Use a mitre saw to cut the $\frac{3}{4}$-inch trim to fit as a frame around each door. Our doors were 4 feet x 8 feet so we cut four 4-foot sections on a 45-degree angle and four 8-foot sections on a 45-degree angle, so that all the angles fit together.

Cut 4 strips of 1-inch x 1-inch trim into 4-foot lengths. This will give you enough trim to create 4 shelves per door. Our shelves were 16 inches deep. Since the trim is 1-inch deep, this will leave approximately 28 inches on the bottom of an 8-foot door. The last piece of trim can be cut to fit from the bottom of the last shelf to the top of the molding on the bottom of the door. You'll need 2 pieces since you have 2 doors.

2

Cut the molding into four 4-foot sections.

We used the top of a round cookie tin to trace two decorative arcs then we cut the arcs out with a jig saw. (Optional)

Prime all the cut pieces of trim and molding as well as the two doors you will be using. When the primer is dry, paint the doors, molding and trim with white paint. When all paint is dry, nail your mitred frame pieces to fit around the edge of each door.

3

Nail the four pieces of 1-inch x 1-inch trim (the shelves) from edge to edge of the door frame, 16 inches down from the top frame. Repeat in 16-inch intervals, so you will have 4 shelves on your door, with a large unused area on the bottom. Repeat this process on the second door.

4

Now that your shelves are in place you are ready to trim the spines from the hardcover books. Use a sharp-edged blade or utility knife to carefully cut the spines off the books. We used approximately 30 spines on each door, but you may wish to use more to give a fuller appearance.

(CONTINUED NEXT PAGE)

HOW TO **FAUX BOOKSHELF** (CONT)

Use a glue gun to affix the spines to the shelves. To give the shelves a more natural appearance, don't line up all the spines in a row across each shelf. Instead, space the books out, some leaning on each other, some placed vertically on top of each other. Mix up the colours and sizes of the spines to achieve the look you like best.

When all the spines are glued in place, you are ready to nail your molding to the top and bottom of each door.

The molding must be flush to the top and bottom edge of each door, so the door is able to swing open easily.

Nail the last piece of trim vertically in the middle of the empty space at the bottom of the door to create a two-door cupboard look. Repeat this process on the second closet door.

Attach two door handles to your new "cupboard" (one on each side of the middle piece of trim). Repeat this process on the second closet door.

Attach the other door handles, one on each closet door at the second shelf level. These will be the real handles for your closet doors, so make sure they are secure.

The last step is a quick tea stain on the white exposed areas above and around the book spines on each shelf. Simply steep a tea bag until the liquid is a strong, dark colour. Remove the tea bag and use a small paintbrush to paint the stain over the white paint until the desired effect is achieved.

Hang your new doors in the closet.

DAY 2

PAINTING Day Two, time to start painting stripes. David mixed one part Textureline bronze metallic paint with one part long-drying glaze. "We have a nice open period, about one hour, to work with this," he explained. Sarah would do the rolling and Janet was to follow to do the stippling. "Don't put the glaze on too thick and you don't need to apply much pressure," David advised. Janet's job was to remove the roller marks. "You want to try to keep your brush flat," David said.

FAUX BOOKSHELF Then it was Renée's turn. "David, I was told you have a job for me." "We're using these doors as faux bookshelves," he explained. "I'd like you to glue the book spines on the shelves to complete the look." "What a great visual trick," she said. David showed her how to begin by gluing the first book spine into the corner. "Place the other spines on the shelf in a pleasing manner," he said. "There doesn't have to be any rhyme or reason. Put some books horizontally, some vertically. Mix colours and sizes. We don't have enough to do solid bookcases. Use your imagination," he said.

MOLDING Renée got creative, gluing about 30 spines to each door. When she was finished, Graeme attached molding to the top and bottom edge of each door to give the faux bookcases a finished look. He also created faux cupboards at the bottom of the doors by nailing trim to the middle of the bottom section and attaching doors. (See how-to box.)

AFTER THE FAUX BOOKSHELF REALLY MAKES THE ROOM SPECIAL

FINISHING TOUCHES Janet had some extra metallic paint so she painted the light fixture to match the walls. With one hour to go until this library would be open for business, a comfortable leopard print chair David had bought was set in one corner and the two real bookshelves were filled with framed photos and books.

THE RESULT The finished space was warm, cozy and inviting. As Renée said, "We turned a lacklustre landing into a literary lounge."

BUDGET

Chair and Ottoman	$550.00	Old Books	$65.00
Pillars	$65.00	Glaze	$23.00
		TOTAL (EXCLUDING PAINT)	**$703.00**

THE CHALLENGE Charlene and Dale Willard had a small room off their bedroom that was used mainly for storage and sometimes as a place where Charlene could do some sewing. But she was going back to school in the fall and needed a home office. The only condition the Willards placed on the renovation was that the dark blue carpet, which had been recently laid, would be retained.

HOMEWORK FOR AN

THE GOAL Create a cozy study retreat out of a small, dark room.

THE TEAM Next-door neighbours Denise and James Turner, working with designer Alison Koski and carpenter Jason Kuczeryk.

OFFICE

THE SOLUTION The room had lots of potential, said Alison. "It would make a great home office but it also had to be flexible enough to meet Charlene and Dale's changing needs later on. I didn't want to create something that would be too permanent, not strictly office nor strictly sitting room."

BEFORE THE WALLPAPER HAD TO GO!   AFTER A BRIGHT SUNNY WORKSPACE

DAY 1

WALLS To create a relaxing environment, Alison wanted to use taupes and tans on the walls. She planned to pick up the blue in the rug with a fabric she found that included all three colours and could be used for cushions and a window seat. First step, the dark blue wallpaper had to go. Sounds good, right? Wrong.

WHOOPS What Alison didn't realize was that the wallpaper had been applied directly to the original drywall without any prep coat. A wallpaper prep coat is a solution you roll on your walls that seals the walls, much like a primer before painting. Unfortunately, that step had been skipped in this instance, which meant that the wallpaper wouldn't peel off smoothly, stubbornly resisting the valiant efforts of Denise and James as they battled with a steamer and scrapers. But because drywall is really only plasterboard sandwiched with paper and because plaster is made with water, it can become soft when using a steamer. It's almost like reactivating the plaster when you steam it too much.

REMOVING WALLPAPER In retrospect, said Alison, she should have tested the wall by scoring the paper very gently with a paper tiger, a tool that makes tiny perforated holes in the paper without damaging the drywall. Then she would have sprayed a bit of fabric softener and water on the scored area and with a wide putty knife attempted to peel back some of the paper. If it comes off easily, there's not going to be a problem. If it doesn't, one should be prepared to work patiently, using a steamer sparingly on the wallpaper.

DRYWALL That's what Denise and James had to rely on as they steamed and scraped and scraped and steamed. By the end of Day One, the rug was covered with scraps of wallpaper but the walls were bare. They were also nicked in places. Thank goodness for Jason, who professionally took over to apply drywall compound, smoothing the walls and letting them dry overnight so they could be painted the next day. That evening the word "wallpaper" could not be uttered near Alison, Denise or James. And this was supposed to be fun.

DAY 2

PAINT Day Two started slightly behind schedule but everyone was rested and back on the job. Denise got to work applying CIL Dulux latex gloss Bramble Tan (10YY 48/071) to the walls with Natural White latex gloss trim (50YY 83/029). Jason, with help from James, was building a pine harvest table-style desk.

DESK They all agreed that the room shouldn't look too much like a home office with a traditional metal desk. Instead, it would be warmed with wood. Alison decided on a table rather than a desk with drawers because that meant that papers would have to be filed away. "I didn't want a big brown box in the corner of the room, I wanted something that would float a little. I wanted to create a romantic environment that was part office and part sitting area."

AFTER THE HARVEST TABLE PROVIDES AMPLE ROOM TO WORK

SHELVES Once the the desk was finished, Jason got busy with a shelving unit to match. That helped balance the room, said Alison, as did taupe curtains on the windows that complemented the taupe walls. Alison cut a piece of foam to fit the window seat Jason had made. She then used her fabric find to cover the seat and recover the two chair cushions from Charlene's white wicker chairs.

ARMOIRE An armoire that Alison had bought added some vertical interest to the room. It was stained a darker wood tone than the pine to give it oomph but not make it the centre of attention.

THE RESULT Despite the size of the room, the finished renovation had many visual focal points — the desk in the corner, the wicker chairs on either side of the shelving unit and the cozy window seat. In the end, despite the nightmare wallpaper episode, the room worked well. Charlene and Dale were delighted and Alison thought everything came together nicely. Alison says when she determines a design plan for any room she looks at what is permanent, what cannot be changed (in this case the blue carpet) and then chooses a colour palette that she can coordinate to make the room pop.

AFTER **INVITING SEATING AREA**

BUDGET				
Wood, Stain	$405.62	Chair Pad	$41.05
Accessories	$125.00	Desk Chair and Lamp	$23.00
Hardware	$117.44	Candle Holder	$21.00
Fabric	$78.82	Candle Holders (second hand)	$15.00
Armoire (second hand)	$70.00	Wheat Sheaf (second hand)	$10.00
		Carpenter's Expenses	$51.20
		TOTAL (EXCLUDING PAINT)	**$958.13**

THE CHALLENGE Shelley White and Sean Stanleigh have a second floor room that used to be a kitchen, with kitchen cupboards and a linoleum floor. They added a bookcase and a chair, but were really thinking of it as an appropriate place for a bar. Mostly, it was bare and depressing. "A sad sack of a room," said Shelley. They avoided it because they didn't know how to use it. What they wanted, they decided, was a room in which they could hang out, read and entertain. "Something with a little bit of funkiness that you wouldn't see in an average home," Sean explained.

CREATING A RETRO

THE GOAL To create a lounge with an eclectic sensibility and, since Shelley and Sean collect retro items, a retro feel.

THE TEAM Shelley and Sean's friends, Kate Stewart and Bret Dawson, with designer Erica Swanson and carpenter Graeme Kelly.

LOUNGE

THE SOLUTION Erica knew that Shelley and Sean didn't want country charm, flowery chintz or boring neutrals. She originally planned something retro and hip, orange and cream perhaps, but then she discovered that the whole first floor of the house was orange. She said, "I suppose that was a good thing. I was, after all, on the right track. But now what? Since the room would be seen mainly in the evening, I decided to play with the lighting and dimensions. I have always found that when someone tries to make a tiny room look bigger, it ends up looking just like someone trying to make a tiny room look bigger." The effect that she was after was a smoky barroom and what better way to reflect that than with a dark, rich colour? So Erica chose CIL Dulux Manor House, (50 YR 08/038-6) a smoky dark brown for the walls, Silver Mink (50 YR 33/040-8), a silvery cream for the cabinets and counter, and Snow Princess (00YY 73/035-7) as a white accent for ceiling and baseboards. "Snow Princess," Bret remarked. "Sean's going to love that."

BEFORE & AFTER **IN NEED OF AMBIANCE...NOW IT'S READY TO RHUMBA!**

DAY 1

CABINETRY While Kate and Erica prepared to paint, Bret removed the upper cabinet doors and Graeme began building an extension to the kitchen counter to fill the space and cover the small bar fridge that was already in place.

COLOUR Renée was surprised when Kate began rolling on the brown paint. But Kate was confident. "Sean and Shelley are so much into colour. You just have to look at the rest of their house," she said. "This will be like a dark hotel bar." Erica showed Kate that the countertop could be painted once it was sanded and a good stain-control primer had been applied. The countertop would require two coats of paint.

CHAIRS Bret was busy painting two reclaimed wooden armchairs white and then fitting them with dark brown seat cushions. Renée and Erica wrestled with another chair, trying to slip on a white slipcover and Kate continued her work on the cupboards.

PAINT When everybody finally put down their paintbrushes, the changes were obvious. "A paintastic day," said Renée. "And so much more," added Bret.

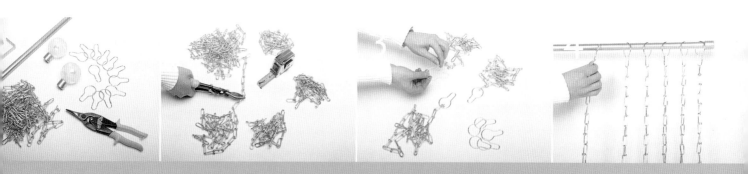

HOW TO CHAIN WINDOW TREATMENT

curtain rod to fit the window with hardware to attach

high-tech or funky finials (we used crystal balls from Ikea)

wire cutter

simple silver shower curtain rings (enough to span the rod with 1/2 inch between each ring)

silver metal chain link — lots of it

Decide where you would like to hang the rod.

Install hardware.

Measure from the rod to the floor.

Cut the chain link into pieces equal to the length from the rod to the floor.

Hook them to the shower curtain hooks and then hang on rod.

Place rod on hardware.

AFTER **A PERFECT CORNER FOR ENTERTAINING**

DAY 2

FABRIC Day Two began with Bret giving the new countertop a coat of silver mink paint while Graeme worked on new bookshelves. Erica got to work at her sewing machine with the brown fabric she had bought on sale, hemming a skirt that would wrap around the edge of the countertop to hide the bar fridge.

FLOOR Now the focus was on the dull and scuffed floor. Erica had found inexpensive peel-and-stick floor tiles that were easily applied over the existing linoleum. She had also planned to hang glass beads at the window to glitter as they caught the light, but couldn't find what she had in mind. Then she thought of hardware store chain. Perfect. Bret trimmed these chains to fit the window. A decorative rod and finials completed the look. Not only would this finished treatment allow in lots of light, it would sparkle when the sun went down. (See how-to box, previous page.)

FINISHING TOUCHES The final touch was to add some whimsy. Renée was delegated to glam up inexpensive drinking glasses (12 for $4.99) by gluing on coloured glass marbles. The glasses were displayed in the open cupboards. Graeme made an autograph board by cutting a sheet of MDF and jig sawing out a square in the middle. (See how-to box.) Erica filled the frame with quotes commemorating when Sean and Shelley met, when they married, when they bought the house and finally this "decorating challenge." She left enough room for party goers to include their own comments. "It's what I call a living art frame," she explained.

BUDGET

Furniture	$386.91	Fabric	$34.49
Window Chain	$181.37	Matting for Frames	$15.09
Tiles	$125.83	Marbles	$9.18
Glasses	$60.00	Carpenter's Expenses	$77.39
Sewing Materials	$17.05		
		TOTAL (EXCLUDING PAINT)	**$907.31**

THE RESULT The transformation was completed with not a penny to spare. But the desired look had been achieved. What was once a white bare and spare room was now a moody hangout, just great for entertaining. "My rule about design," said Erica, "is that rules are made to be broken. If there is one basic doctrine that I can offer, it's that you can never go wrong if you make decisions with your heart. A room will inevitably come together if you fill it with the things you love."

HOW TO HANGING AUTOGRAPH BOARD

1

one 12-inch x 18-inch piece of white art board

one fine point felt tipped marker or calligraphy pen

one 12-inch x 18-inch picture frame

one quart of amber paint, or another complementary colour

one small paint brush

one tube of white latex caulking

one caulking gun

2

Paint the picture frame and set aside to dry. We used an amber colour, but you could use any colour that complements your walls.

While the frame is drying you will have time to prepare the art board. We used a black marker to write some quotes on the board that had special meaning. Make sure you leave lots of room for guests to write their names or comments on the board.

When the writing is complete, attach the art board to the back of the dry frame.

3
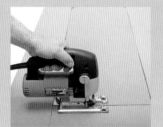

We used white caulking to create some interesting patterns on the frame. When the caulking is dry you may paint it in a complementary colour or just let it remain white.

With your design complete, your autograph board is now ready to hang.

THE CHALLENGE Teenagers Lindsay and Deirdre Magrane wanted a funky place to hang out with their friends. The family rec room used to be a playroom filled with their toys, but now it looked stodgy, drab and dark. It was a cold basement, definitely not a cool destination. Marion, Lindsay and Deirdre's mother, was delighted that her daughters were caught up in this decorating mode.

A HOT TEENAGE

THE GOAL Spruce up the rec room, add storage space and bright colours.

THE TEAM Next-door neighbours, teenagers Michael and Jocelyn Butler, who had a vested interest in improving the space since they spend a lot of time there. They were joined by their mother, Pat Butler, designer Catherine Pavlovich and carpenter Bill Crossman.

HANGOUT

THE SOLUTION The room was long and narrow, with a fireplace in the middle of one wall, a garage door at one end and the TV at the other end. Catherine said the shape of the room made rearranging the furniture impossible but the relatively large size meant that she could get away with a lot of colours. She chose a colour scheme using CIL Dulux shades of Larkspur Purple (06RB 24/258), Meadowgrass (5C14-3) and Enamel Blue (5C2-6). The purple and green would be for the walls, the blue for the fireplace, window trim and doors. She also found some fun fabric for window treatments and cushions and decreed that the old beige rug would have to go. Royal blue carpeting would be used instead.

BEFORE THE 70S ARE OVER...   AFTER WELCOME TO THE FUTURE

DAY 1

WALLS The first step was to paint the walls. Since there was already old wallpaper that had been applied directly to the drywall, they decided to glue down any peeling areas and paint directly on top of the paper. The walls were primed and then Michael and Jocelyn began painting them purple and green. It was about this time that Catherine learned about Marion's aversion to purple. "That's okay," said Michael as he splashed on some more purple. "This room is for the girls. Marion doesn't come downstairs anyway."

BOOKCASE Pat and Bill were building floor-to-ceiling bookcases, like open boxes stacked on top of each other, with biscuit joints holding everything together. The bookcases were primed and the painting crew took over to colour them green. Finally, they were set on either side of the fireplace against the purple wall. Meanwhile, the facing wall was going green with a wave of blue. Purple spirals would be added later. Catherine's goal was to leave no surface unpainted, to add as much colour as she could, and banish the word "beige."

> BEFORE & AFTER FROM MIXED-UP AND MESSY TO CLEAN AND WELL-ORGANIZED

HOW TO DECORATED MIRROR

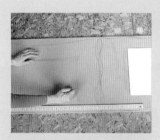

1

sheet of MDF

pencil and ruler

design template

jig saw

router and bits

drill with bits

sandpaper

hot glue gun and glue sticks

paint and paint brushes

small roller with sleeve and tray

beads and baubles to dress up the mirror

mirror

silicone sealant

caulking gun

picture hanging kit

2

3

4

MDF comes in 4-foot x 8-foot sheets. Have the lumberyard cut it in half lengthwise.

Draw or trace the design you would like straight onto the board. Make sure that you measure the mirror before drawing the inside cut-out. This hole should be at least 1 inch smaller than the mirror all the way around.

Once the pattern is perfect cut out the design using a jig saw.

To cut out the interior, first drill a hole in the cut-out and then jig saw out the shape that you want.

Using a roll-over bit, rout all the edges to give a finished look.

Sand and paint in the colour of your choice.

Once dry, embellish the mirror around the cut-out by gluing on the beads and baubles with the glue gun.

Let the glue dry.

To attach the mirror, caulk out a thick bead of silicone sealant around the back of the cut-out. Carefully place the mirror and apply pressure until it starts to hold. Let dry.

Attach the hanging apparatus and hang your decorative mirror.

DAY 2

PAINT Day Two and the paint brigade was on the march. Jocelyn was carefully painting a picture frame fuchsia. The next step would be to trim it with silk flowers. An old coffee table was getting updated as Bill replaced the old-fashioned legs with a new set that were painted purple. The tabletop was painted blue and then got up with green spirals, stencilled on to match the spirals on the walls.

FLOOR Now it was time to rug and roll. The old carpet was cut up and removed, the new blue one rolled into place. Matching blue fabric was hemmed for slipcovers to disguise the old couches.

AFTER THE COMPLETED LAMP AND SHADE   AFTER A GREAT PLACE TO HANG OUT

FINISHING TOUCHES Catherine turned a sad, old brown lamp into a fluorescent wonder with a blue base and green fabric featuring a feathery green marabou for the shade. (See how-to box.) The fireplace mantel was also getting the blue treatment while pillows for the couches were quickly stitched and then thrown into place. Purple curtains bordered with silk flowers were hung on the windows and funky, decorated mirrors were hung on the wall. (See how-to box, previous page.)

BUDGET

Carpet	$360.00	Curtain Rods	$19.52
Fabric for Cushions	$99.47	Cushion	$13.50
Accent Paint	$56.32	Fabric for Curtains	$8.05
Fabric for Couch	$51.52	Glass Beads	$7.82
Floor Lamp	$46.98	Lampshade	$5.59
Cushion Forms	$41.68	Small Table	$5.40
Art Supplies	$19.95	Carpenter's Expenses	$149.75
		TOTAL (EXCLUDING PAINT)	**$885.55**

THE RESULT Almost everything that didn't move went under the paintbrush, with the participants getting their fair share of paint on them too. But it was worth it because a room that had formerly been dull and dreary was now exploding with colour and hip designs. Lindsay and Deirdre couldn't believe the transformation. Marion loved the room, too — including the colour purple.

HOW TO A FUNKY, FEMININE LAMP

1

plain lamp shade

enough fabric to cover the lamp shade

maribou/feather boa to go around base of shade

spray adhesive

school glue

2

Trace an outline of the lamp shade and cut the fabric to size.

Attach the fabric to the shade using spray adhesive. Glue any ends onto the inside of the shade using white school glue. Let dry.

Using glue gun, attach maribou to bottom of lamp shade. Let dry.

Assemble lamp base, bulb, and shade.

3

4

5

THE CHALLENGE Leighann and Al Paulionis had a bleak, bare, basement laundry room. It wasn't the kind of place you'd want to spend a lot of time, not that most people really want to spend much time in their laundry rooms. But there was no storage space and it shared the basement with the pipes and furnace. "It was awful down there and definitely a place that we couldn't have handled alone," said Leighann.

LIGHTENING UP THE

THE GOAL Separate the laundry room from the rest of the basement, brighten it and add usable storage facilities plus a counter for folding. Al says he's pretty good at folding. Leighann says she's better at refolding what Al has folded. Leighann was specific that she didn't want a room with loons or cow themes, but aside from that she just hoped for a cheerful space.

THE TEAM Old friends Patricia McEntee-Dunne and Patrick Dunne with designer Riva Glogowski and carpenter Genia Fromme.

LAUNDRY

THE SOLUTION Riva knew she wanted to divide the room from the rest of the basement, but with the limited budget and time putting up drywall was not an option. She decided to use colour and fabric instead. The first step was finding a cheery blue fabric that would set the theme for the room. CIL Dulux Blue Stemware, a latex eggshell (30BB55/152-7), was chosen as the colour for the walls, complementing the fabric, and a white concrete paint was selected for the floor.

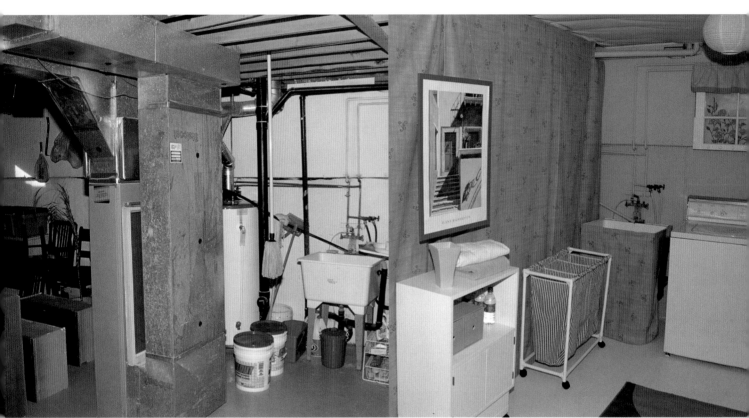

BEFORE **DINGY AND UNFINISHED**   AFTER **FRESH AND CLEAN**

DAY 1

WALLS Patricia and Patrick began priming, with two coats, mindful that this was a damp area, allowing enough time for each coat to dry thoroughly before painting the walls, again with two coats. Meanwhile, Riva and Genia discovered old kitchen cabinets in another part of the basement that they decided they could recycle with the addition of a new countertop.

CABINETS Once the walls were painted, it was time to work on the cabinets with CIL Dulux White Mountain latex eggshell (50BB83/020). To relate the white cabinets to the blues in the room, the doors were removed and CIL Dulux Flo Blue (30BB 14/277-6), also a latex eggshell, was used to outline the cabinet door panels. Then a potato stamp, which gives a hand-painted look rather than a regular stencil, was applied with the blue paint to add a *fleur de lis* pattern. (See how-to box.) The doors were then reattached and dressed up with new handles. By the end of the first day, you could say this team had a good handle on things.

AFTER UNSIGHTLY STORAGE SPACE SOLVED!

HOW TO USING A POTATO STAMP

1

a couple of potatoes

artist's acrylic colours/coloured inks/acrylic latex paint

wallpaper paste

water

a sharp knife

sharp cutting tools for cutting details ("U"- and "V"- shaped small gouges)

scalpel (with spare blades)

a felt pen/sable brush

a soft, square-ended artist's brush and/or small roller

2

Cut the potato in half using one decisive stroke. The potato half must be flat!

Remove excess moisture by pressing the potato firmly onto a piece of paper towel.

Using the felt pen/sable brush, sketch out your motif.

3

Cut out the motif. Use your scalpel, cutting around the motif first, angling the blade slightly to give a bevelled edge. It's important not to undercut, as this weakens the stamp. Use the gouges to cut details.

Once your motif is cut out, apply colour to the potato using a roller or brush. This will give you a clean, crisp and more controlled image. (Otherwise, you could end up with splats and smudges.) Press firmly onto the surface that you want to stamp.

4

5

DAY 2

WINDOW TREATMENT Day Two in the basement was looking brighter, but Riva planned to add some scenery as well. She had found a garage sale window that offered a vista of imaginative opportunities. The frame was painted white and then Patrick painted clouds on the walls and a glorious trail of morning glories. (See how-to box.) Once the frame was fixed to the wall, a picture of the family cat peering into the room was stuck in one pane, and a curtain valance was hung overtop. This gave the room a focus and now it felt less confined.

FINISHING TOUCHES The blue fabric was quickly hemmed and everyone pitched in to drape it from hooks on the beams, partitioning off the laundry area. Because the partition was fabric, the other areas of the basement are still easily accessible. After that, the ceiling, with its exposed pipes, was covered with inexpensive white muslin, using staples to attach the muslin to the ceiling. "It was tricky but it worked," said Riva. "Drywall would have been the best way to cover up the ceiling area, but we could only afford fabric."

HOW TO PAINT CLOUDS ON YOUR WALLS

primer

blue satin finish paint

white semi-gloss paint

glaze

full-size paint roller

4-inch paint roller

2-inch paint brush

paint tray

The first step in the cloud-painting process is to prepare the walls for paint. Use the 2-inch brush to prime the crevice between the ceiling and the walls and between each wall. Then use the paint roller to prime the rest of the walls. You may find it easier to go over the wall next to the crevices with the small paint roller. Give the walls 2 coats of primer, allowing each coat to dry thoroughly.

After the primer, apply 2 coats of blue paint and allow to dry thoroughly. At the same time, paint a piece of board or wallboard; this will be used to practice your cloud-painting technique.

Mix the glaze and the white paint, using a 4-to-1 ratio. Mix thoroughly and pour into paint tray. Continue to mix this several times while you are painting as the mixture has a tendency to separate.

Choose a piece of sponge, wet it, and wring it out completely. Next, dab it into the white paint, then dab on the ridges of the paint tray to remove excess paint.

With your sponge, start dabbing on the board in a fairly straight line for the bottom of the cloud. Then start dabbing paint above this line, twisting and turning the sponge as you dab, to build your cloud. When you are satisfied with the general shape of the cloud, take your damp cheesecloth and dab gently over the entire cloud, softening the paint

THE RESULT Riva said that if the budget had allowed extra spending, she would have bought more fake greenery for the room. As it was, the finished effect was clean and bright. Leighann and Al were more than pleased. Patricia suggested that they could even hold a party in this new, inviting room.

The renovations came in within the $1,000 budget. If Leighann and Al ever choose to completely renovate the basement, Riva said the fabric can be recycled and used somewhere else.

BUDGET

Fabric	$341.27	Plants	$25.69
Laundry Bag	$93.67	Craft Supplies	$20.27
Counter	$70.15	Window (second hand)	$10.00
Lamps	$51.63	Carpenter's Expenses	$139.96
Laundry Accessories	$35.43		
		TOTAL (EXCLUDING PAINT)	**$788.07**

pieces of sea sponge, big enough to be held between your thumb and fingers

a piece of cheesecloth, about 18 inches x 24 inches

a piece of board or wallboard, approximately 36 inches x 24 inches

and giving it a more cloud-like appearance. You may then dab a few more bits of paint on the cloud, towards the centre, to add some texture. You will create each cloud in the same way, twisting and turning and dabbing the sponge, softening with the cheesecloth, and then adding texture with a few more dabs of paint. Practise until you're happy with the results.

Find the middle of the largest wall, both vertically and horizontally — just eyeball it. Then, move to either your left or right about a foot. Go up or down about a foot from the vertical centre that you found. This is where you will begin painting. This is an important step because it will eliminate the effect of a bulls-eye — a cloud painted right in the middle of the wall! Make your largest cloud about 20–24 inches in length, medium clouds 10–15 inches, small 5–10 inches, and wisps as small as 2 inches. (These sizes are based on a room of about 8 feet x 10 feet. If your room is larger or smaller, adjust your sizes appropriately.)

Wrap some of your clouds around the corners of the walls and start some right from the baseboards or window trim. Don't forget to paint small wisps of clouds around light switches, electrical outlets, cool air vents, and wall-mounted lights. These details really pay off!

DESIGNERS

KAREN ADLER KAREN ADLER DESIGNS

Karen Adler says she has mastered the art of bargain shopping. She frequents antique shows, auctions and discount outlets to bring her clients "bang for their buck!"

ELLIE CHOLETTE AT HOME INTERIOR DESIGN

As the owner of At Home Interior Design, Ellie Cholette's philosophy includes the three Rs: recycling, restyling and reusing.

EVELYN ESHUN EVELYN: DESIGN

Evelyn Eshun says her goal is to create environments for her clients that will relax, inspire and speak volumes about their own style.

OREET FAGAN INTERIORS BY OREET

Oreet Fagan says working with budgets does not mean having to sacrifice ingenuity and good design. She's been known to add whimsical items to a room that will put a smile on your face.

RIVA GLOGOWSKI COTTINGHAM DESIGN HOUSE

An interior decorator with a wide range of specialities, Riva Glogowski can tackle everything from total home décor to room rearrangements with a fresh eye.

JAN KERR DESIGNER HOUSE CALLS INC.

Jan Kerr enjoys creating one-of-a-kind interiors and believes homes should be functional, comfortable and sometimes even a little quirky.

ALISON KOSKI RETRO RECOVERIES

Alison Koski's specialty is mixing the old with the new — whether it's a great find that needs some love or an antique looking for a new home.

TRACY KUNDELL AVALON INTERIORS

Tracy Kundell is an experienced and visionary designer with a knack for providing clients with interiors that reflect and enhance their personality and lifestyle.

DAVID MACPHEE DAVID MACPHEE DESIGN SERVICES LIMITED

David MacPhee's mission statement is to interpret the dreams of clients and make them a reality. He does this regularly on *The Decorating Challenge*.

CHRISTINE NEWELL CHRISTINE NEWELL INTERIOR DÉCOR

Christine Newell says "Every project is an enjoyable challenge. And no matter what the budget, any room can be transformed!"

CATHERINE PAVLOVICH CATWORKS

Catherine Pavlovich is a skilled artist whose interior decorating background stems from a love of painting and transforming plain interiors.

MICHELLE PETRIE MICHELLE PETRIE INTERIORS

Michelle Petrie has been in the design business for 14 years. Her strength is achieving the desired result at remarkably little cost.

TAMMY SCHNURR TILLOW BY DESIGN

Tammy Schnurr believes recycling is a responsibility and she demonstrates this in her designs by mixing the old with the new to create affordable, original style that complements any home.

ERICA SWANSON TORONTO DESIGNERS

Erica Swanson believes in creating a space for her clients that flows through their individualism and surrounds them with what they love.

MICHAEL VUXSTA HOME OUTFITTERS

Michael Vuxsta is not concerned with creating fashionable furniture or interiors but with creating contemporary, comfortable and lasting designs.

ADRIANA URTASUN

Adriana Urtasun is a designer who is known for her artistic sensibility. She applies her sensitivity to colour and composition to both commercial and residential spaces.

CARPENTERS

BILL CROSSMAN

Bill Crossman's expertise as a professional contractor comes in handy on the show. Even under pressure, he always seems to keep calm, cool and collected which isn't always easy on *The Decorating Challenge*.

GRAEME KELLY

Graeme Kelly brings much more to the show than just that big smile. He's been honing his contracting skills for over 15 years and he's always up for a challenge.

JEREMY PLANT

"No problem" is the most common response designers hear from Jeremy Plant. No matter how busy life gets, he never complains. His active lifestyle includes working on *The Decorating Challenge* and managing a home renovation centre.

PAUL TREBILCOCK

Paul Trebilcock lists his three main interests as hand tools, power tools and air tools. He loves the fact that *The Decorating Challenge* gives him the opportunity to use these tools as "weapons of mass construction."